THE DONNE TRADITION

THE
DONNE
TRADITION

A STUDY IN ENGLISH POETRY FROM
DONNE TO THE DEATH OF COWLEY

BY

GEORGE WILLIAMSON

OCTAGON BOOKS

A DIVISION OF FARRAR, STRAUS AND GIROUX

New York   1973

Copyright © 1930 by the President and Fellows of Harvard College
Copyright © 1958 by George Williamson

Reprinted 1973

OCTAGON BOOKS
A Division of Farrar, Straus & Giroux, Inc.
19 Union Square West
New York, N. Y. 10003

Library of Congress Cataloging in Publication Data

Williamson, George, 1898-1968.
    The Donne tradition; *a study in English poetry from Donne
    to the death of Cowley. see dip*
    Reprint of the ed. published by Noonday Press, New York, which
    was issued as N127 of Noonday paperbacks.

    ~~Bibliography: p.~~
    1. English poetry—Early modern (to 1700)—History and criti-
    cism.   2. Donne, John, 1572-1631.   I. Title.
PR545.M4W5   1973   821'.3'09   73-12738
ISBN 0-374-98632-0

Printed in USA by
Thomson-Shore,Inc.
Dexter, Michigan

FOR

MY MOTHER AND FATHER

But, though all knowledge be in those Authors already, yet, as some poisons, and some medicines, hurt not, nor profit, except the creature in which they reside, contribute their lively activitie, and vigor; so, much of the knowledge buried in Books perisheth, and becomes ineffectuall, if it be not applied, and refreshed by a companion, or friend. — DONNE

PREFACE

THIS book was really begun in a small essay on "The Talent of T. S. Eliot," which appeared in *The Sewanee Review*. There I urged the relationship of Eliot to Donne, only to find myself beguiled into larger speculations. In short, I became absorbed in the Donne tradition through a contemporary poet.

But my debt to Mr. Eliot goes beyond enticement. His critical thinking on the "metaphysical poets" has so influenced my own that I can only express my deep obligation to him, without trying to define its limits. To him also I owe the courtesy of reading part of my book in manuscript.

At length, while attempting to make my position clear on the Metaphysical poets, I acquired a special indebtedness to the profound scholarship of Professor W. D. Briggs and to the provocative criticism of Professor H. D. Gray.

Moreover, no one can write of the Metaphysical poets without avowing an obligation to the splendid editions of seventeenth-century poets published by the Oxford University Press — especially to Saintsbury's *Caroline Poets*, Grierson's *Donne*, Margoliouth's *Marvell*, and Martin's *Crashaw* and *Vaughan*. For particular praise every student of Donne must single out Professor Grierson's memorable edition. The discriminating reader cannot fail to see what I owe to my predecessors, and in what I have fallen short of their labors.

I should be less than truthful if I did not express regret that M. Pierre Legouis's *André Marvell* and *Donne the Craftsman* came too late for my book to profit by his researches. Had they come earlier, some of my argument might have been bolstered, some shaped to meet a new disagreement. I must also express my admiration of the exceedingly able criticism which Signor Mario Praz has contributed to the study of seventeenth-century poets, both in his *Secentismo e Marinismo in Inghilterra* and in his reviews of other books.

For courteous permission to reprint some parts of this book, I have to thank the editors of *Modern Language Notes*, *The Sewanee Review*, and *Studies in Philology*.

There remains the pleasure of acknowledging the gracious assistance of my wife, Jehanne de Laincel, who has read and criticized the proof-sheets.

Decency requires me to add that, with such guidance and support, the faults are mine.

G. W.

University of Oregon
    October, 1929

CONTENTS

THE DONNE TRADITION

I. JOHN DONNE AND
HIS SHROUD

OF ALL English poets John Donne was probably the most profoundly haunted by the thought of death. In his self-revealing *Biathanatos* he says: "Mee thinks I have the keyes of my prison in mine own hand, and no remedy presents it selfe so soon to my heart, as mine own sword." [1] Death was his symbol of deliverance from life, but it was a symbol at once terrible and fascinating. Death was the mistress of his philosophy and the winding-sheet of his final peace. If his youth gives us the roses and his age the yew of the Renascence, it is with the savage, mystic, and sensual intensity which brought a death's-head to his love and a premature shroud to his last illness. Though he sometimes forgot the worm in the rose, from cradle to grave he never "allayed the fever of the bone."

Especially in this morbidity, Donne reminds us of Baudelaire, for his own poems brought to the dying Elizabethan age the sharper flavor of *Les Fleurs du Mal.* In fact, the study of Baudelaire is a preparation that no one should neglect who would get the most out of Donne. In a rather misguided sense, both were poets of an age of decadence, and have therefore been called decadent poets. Both were haunted

1. Cited by Grierson, *Donne's Poetical Works*, ii, 270.

by the desire to escape from this world; and both wrote poetry which surprises, shocks, and baffles expectation, with metallic music and rebellious emotion. If we understand the sensibility which moulds *De Profundis Clamavi* or such lines as

> Et le Temps m'engloutit minute par minute,
> Comme la neige immense un corps pris de roideur;
> Je contemple d'en haut le globe en sa rondeur,
> Et je n'y cherche plus l'abri d'une cahute!

from *Le Gout du Néant*, we shall understand Donne better. Besides a certain kinship in their mode of feeling, we shall find that their images have a similar faculty of opening novel and bizarre vistas of emotion. Both Donne and Baudelaire were fascinated by the ugly, and both combined mental and physical anguish in the thought of death.

The more I study Donne the more I am persuaded that Walton has given us the essential facts, although he has taken a dejected and discomposed soul and charmed it into sweet and quiet thoughts. In his singularly charming *Life of Dr. John Donne* I find "those greater facts which mould and colour all the artist's work." To these facts I wish to give a new, and I hope a truer, emphasis; to take from them that "unexpressible addition of comeliness" which softens their vigorous meaning. If by robbing Walton of his charm I may give greater truth to his picture, perhaps I may be pardoned the lamentable loss.[1]

---

1. For my facts and quotations I draw upon Walton's *Life*, corrected in some details by Gosse and Grierson.

In Elizabethan documentary accounts, Shakspere and Donne make their appearance at the same time, the year 1592. Shakspere was twenty-eight and Donne was nineteen. He had just been entered at Lincoln's Inn, and the future lay bright before him, for already he had been hailed as another Pico Mirandola. Even then he must have presented the character which Walton gives us:

He was of stature moderately tall, of a straight and equally proportioned body, to which all his words and actions gave an unexpressible addition of comeliness.

The melancholy and pleasant humour were in him so contempered, that each gave advantage to the other, and made his company one of the delights of mankind.

His fancy was unimitably high, equalled only by his great wit; both being made useful by a commanding judgment.

His aspect was cheerful, and such as gave a silent testimony of a clear knowing soul, and of a conscience at peace with itself. . . .

He was by nature highly passionate, but more apt to reluct at the excesses of it.

In truth, Donne must have had great charm, but there was more in him than met the eye, even of Walton.

The young man who thus presented himself at Lincoln's Inn had in his veins the blood of John Heywood and Sir Thomas More. He had been brought up as a Catholic, had attended both Oxford and Cambridge without taking a degree — because of family objections to the oath of allegiance — and had probably spent some time travelling in Italy and Spain. Now he took up the study of law with an eye to State employment. Meanwhile he became known as "a great Visiter of Ladies, a great Frequenter of Plays, a great Writer of conceited Verses."[1]

But, unlike Shakspere, this young man was peculiarly sensitive to the problems of his day, to the general disintegration of medieval thought and the challenge of the new science, to the religious controversy, to the rival claims of a secular and a sacred calling, and to the relation of such conflicts to his own mind and life. So what time poetry did not steal from law in the years 1593 and 1594 he gave to a careful study "of the body of divinity as it was then controverted betwixt the Reformed and the Roman Church." In 1594, or in his twenty-first year, he showed Rudde, the dean of Gloucester, all the works of Bellarmine, "marked with many weighty observations under his own hand." For such studies his law suffered, since he was, as he says, "diverted by leaving that and embracing the worst voluptuousness, a hydroptic immoderate desire of human learning and languages." This is the view he took when he was in his thirties. Then he had come to regard his beating mind with alarm, and to implore in his *Litanie* that the "Eagle-sighted Prophets" pray for him, lest by their example he excuse his excess

In seeking secrets, or Poëtiquenesse.[2]

Now, however, he must have taken pride in this voluptuousness of mind. For, as Walton tells us, "in

1. Cited by Simpson (*Prose Works of John Donne*, p. 61) from Sir Richard Baker's *Chronicle of the Kings of England*.
2. Grierson, *op. cit.*, i, 341.

the most unsettled days of his youth his bed was not able to detain him beyond the hour of four in a morning; and it was no common business that drew him out of his chamber till past ten, all which time was employed in study, though he took great liberty after it." Then, we may be sure, he put on "his winning behaviour — which, when it would entice, had a strange kind of elegant irresistible art"; then he went out to court the world. Not without reason was it said that this age had brought forth another Pico Mirandola.

The next few years find Donne making several bids for a public career. The first carried him with the Earl of Essex in the expedition to Cadiz in 1596, and again with Essex to the Azores in 1597. The second of these voyages he describes with almost supernatural vividness in *The Storme* and *The Calme*, verse epistles to his Cambridge friend, Christopher Brooke. What his state of mind was at this time, as well as some hint of the years since he came to Lincoln's Inn, may be read in these lines from *The Calme*:

> Whether a rotten state, and hope of gaine,
> Or to disuse mee from the queasie paine
> Of being belov'd, and loving, or the thirst
> Of honour, or faire death, out pusht'mee first,
> I lose my end: for here as well as I
> A desperate may live, and a coward die.[1]

Much is told here. Evidently the experience that he had been adding to his education had begun to make him sick, the three thousand pounds which his father

1. Grierson, *op. cit.*, i, 179.

had left him were spent, and the push of honor or fair
death had become urgent. While this bid for a place
in the sun came to nought, it secured his recommenda-
tion to Sir Thomas Egerton through the kind office of
another young volunteer, the eldest son of this influential statesman.

Sir Thomas Egerton was Lord Keeper of the Great
Seal. Towards the close of 1597 Donne became his
secretary. At last, Donne must have thought, a door
leading to preferment had been opened to him. How
he afterwards regarded it he himself tells us in the
melancholy letter of 1608 in which he deplores that
worst voluptuousness, his immoderate desire for
learning. Admitting this to be a beautiful ornament
for men of great fortune, he continues, "but mine was
grown so low as to need an occupation, which I
thought I entered well into, when I subjected myself
to such a service as I thought might exercise my poor
abilities, and there I stumbled and fell too..." [1]
That stumbling was perhaps the most important single event in his life. Walton seems to have thought
so, but no more than Donne himself.

His marriage was the bitter-sweet occasion of this
stumbling. The lady was Anne More, the niece of Sir
Thomas Egerton's second wife. It was a runaway
marriage, and Anne was not of age. When her father,
Sir George More, discovered it, he had Donne thrown
into prison and dismissed from the service of the
Lord Keeper. And thus the poet's hopes of prefer-

---

1. Quoted by Walton from a letter to Sir Henry Goodyere, *Letters*
(ed. Merrill, 1910), pp. 44-45.

ment were blasted. Donne sent a sad letter to his
wife, and after his signature wrote, "John Donne,
Anne Donne, Un-done."[1] Even this, his deepest love,
had proved "a flattering mischief." But, however he
might condemn himself, he could not regret the love
whose intense feeling was communicated to the most
memorable of his love songs. That splendid elegy
which begins

> By our first strange and fatall interview,

is an eloquent witness to this crisis in his life, and to
the beauty of the love which was returned to him:

> nor in bed fright thy Nurse
> With midnights startings, crying out, oh, oh
> Nurse, o my love is slaine, I saw him goe
> O'r the white Alpes alone.[2]

Although Sir George More was finally reconciled,
and even gave his son-in-law a small allowance, the
damage had been done. And although Sir Thomas
Egerton said, "He parted with a friend, and such a
secretary as was fitter to serve a king than a subject," another door to preferment was closed and evil
days set in for Donne.

From 1601, the date of his marriage, to 1615, the
date of his ordination, he was dependent upon patrons and required to pay a humiliating adulation
which must have irked his proud soul. These were
years darkened by privation, spiritual anguish, and

1. His tender concern for Anne More is most intimately revealed in
Letters (1910), nos. xliv and xlvii.
2. Grierson, *op. cit.*, i, 112–113.

a losing battle to win State preferment. In 1609, the year after he had written *Biathanatos*, he even thought of emigration as a way out of his difficulties, for a contemporary letter tells us "that John Dunn seeks to be Secretary at Virginia." [1] But the Church had already begun to make her advances for the use of his talents. Thomas Morton, Bishop of Durham, approached Donne with these words:

Mr. Donne, I know your education and abilities, I know your expectation of a State employment, and I know your fitness for it, and I know too the many delays and contingencies that attend Court promises. . . . You know I have formerly persuaded you to waive your Court hopes and enter into Holy Orders, which I now again persuade you to embrace.

This he refused to do, in spite of his poverty and his growing family, principally because, as he said, "my present condition is such, that if I ask my own conscience whether it be reconcilable to that rule, it is at this time so perplexed about it, that I can neither give myself nor you an answer." He had not yet reconciled the claims of a religious life with his Renascence temperament and the worldly ambitions of a proud intellect.

Meanwhile he found powerful patrons in Lord Hay, later Earl of Doncaster; Robert Carr, Earl of Somerset; and Sir Robert Drury, whose patronage he gained by his *First Anniversary*, and whose favor took him from Mitcham to London. These patrons were solicitous to the king for some State employment for

1. See Simpson, *Prose Works*, p. 28.

Donne; and according to Walton, "the king had formerly both known and put a value upon his company, and had also given him some hopes of a State employment." Somerset seems to have been especially urgent on Donne's behalf; but, as Walton says, the king denied all requests and replied:

> I know Mr. Donne is a learned man, has the abilities of a learned divine, and will prove a powerful preacher; and my desire is to prefer him that way, and in that way I will deny you nothing for him.

This reply is very characteristic of the pedantic James I, for he and his courtiers, as *The Cambridge History* remarks, "crowded to hear a sermon as an intellectual entertainment." This is hinted in the bitter words of Bishop Andrewes when he said of Ezekiel's contemporaries that

> they seemed to reckon of sermons no otherwise than of songs: to give them the hearing, to commend the aire of them, and so let them goe. The Musike of a song, and the Rhetorique of a sermon, all is one.[1]

But Donne deferred his decision for almost three years. In the meantime he applied himself to an incessant study of textual divinity and the learned languages.

So the times conspired against Donne. The king's words appeared to close forever the door to secular preferment. Nothing remained for him but to take Holy Orders: his Court hopes had been denied. In his letters to Sir Henry Goodyere, we may peer into his

---

1. Cited by *The Cambridge History of English Literature*, iv, 272.

mind during these years of distress. Confessing to an over-earnest desire of the next life, he says:

And though I know it is not merely a weariness of this, because I had the same desire when I went with the tide, and enjoyed fairer hopes than I now do, yet I doubt worldly troubles have increased it; 't is now Spring, and all the pleasures of it displease me; every other tree blossoms, and I wither: I grow older, and not better; my strength diminisheth, and my load grows heavier, and yet I would fain be or do something; but that I cannot tell what, is no wonder in this time of my sadness; for to choose is to do, but to be no part of any body is as to be nothing: and so I am, and shall so judge myself, unless I could be so incorporated into a part of the world as by business to contribute some sustentation to the whole. . . . Sir, I fear my present discontent does not proceed from a good root, that I am so well content to be nothing — that is, dead.[1]

We hear the tones of Hamlet in this passage, the desire to be or do something, the sceptical indecision, the yearning for death as a deliverance. But now he was to enter the Church. And yet religion had always haunted his mind; for had it not always been forced upon his attention — by the fate of his forbears, his early training, his denial of a degree at two universities, and his necessity of disclaiming "love of a corrupt religion" in 1601?

In January of 1615 he was ordained by Bishop King of London. In 1616 he was elected divinity reader at Lincoln's Inn, and there made his reputa-

1. Here Walton combines two letters to Goodyere: *Letters* (1910), nos. xviii and xxvii. Both belong to the year 1608, the close of Shakspere's great tragic period.

tion as a preacher. Then in 1617 his wife died, and he was forced to bury the deepest stay of his life, and to rise to solitary honor with the distant hope of "a bracelet of bright hair about the bone." Once, speaking of the saddest night he ever spent, he says:

> For it exercised those hours, which, with extreme danger to her, whom I should hardly have abstained from recompensing for her company in this world, with accompanying her out of it, encreased my poor family with a son.[1]

In 1621 King James appointed him Dean of St. Paul's, where "always preaching to himself like an angel from a cloud, but in none," he attracted large audiences and rose to his supreme height, for people exclaimed to one another:

> Tell me, had ever pleasure such a dresse,
> Have you knowne crimes so shap'd? or lovelinesse
> Such as his lips did cloth religion in?[2]

At last, late in the summer of 1630, he was stricken down at his daughter's house. Once he rose from his bed to preach the sermon called *Death's Duell* on the first Friday in Lent, 1631. Six weeks later he was dead. People said that he had preached his own funeral sermon.

Shortly before his death he caused his picture to be drawn as it may now be seen in the strange monument which stands in St. Paul's. Walton tells us how an urn and a board were procured, and then a choice

1. *Letters* (1910), p. 127. See also *Holy Sonnets*, no. xvii, for the full power of her influence over him.
2. Chudleigh, *On Dr. John Donne*, Grierson, *op. cit.*, i, 394.

painter to draw his picture, which was taken in this dramatic manner:

Several charcoal fires being first made in his large study, he brought with him into that place his winding-sheet in his hand, and having put off all his clothes, had this sheet put on him, and so tied with knots at his head and feet, and his hands so placed as dead bodies are usually fitted, to be shrouded and put into their coffin or grave. Upon this urn he thus stood, with his eyes shut, and with so much of the sheet turned aside as might show his lean, pale, and death-like face.

This picture was placed by his bedside, where it became his hourly object till death. At the same time he wrote the *Hymne to God my God, in my sicknesse,* which completed his last preparation for death:

Since I am comming to that Holy roome,
    Where, with thy Quire of Saints for evermore,
I shall be made thy Musique; As I come
    I tune the Instrument here at the dore,
    And what I must doe then, thinke here before.

Thus died the English poet whose life and works are most profoundly haunted by the thought of death.

In Walton's portrait of Donne the lines and lights are true, but the shadows are not deep enough. And in these shadows lies the finer truth about him; for instance, the Catholic influence, or the desire for death. Although Donne took up his Anglican duties with all seriousness, his devotional verse shows that his mind never lost the impress of his early Catholic training. The real reason why he was reluctant to take Holy

Orders is also to be found in Walton, but under-em-
phasized: the doubt whether his nature was reconcilable to that rule, for his mind was naturally both
worldly and mystical, and was caught in the welter of
the senses even when seeking secrets. Court hopes
and Holy Orders represented two sides of his nature,
never perhaps wholly reconciled; for, as Walton tells
us, he gave the impression of always preaching to
himself.

Both in his sacred and in his profane experience
there is a spiritualizing progress which derives from a
discipline exerted by one side of his mind over the
other. When his depression was great, he wrote:

> I have not been out of my house since I received your
> pacquet. As I have much quenched my senses, and dis-
> used my body from pleasure, and so tried how I can indure
> to be mine own grave, so I try now how I can suffer a
> prison.[1]

The prison was both his "hospital at Mitcham" and
his own body. In his love, as in his religion, this mental conflict was resolved by a compromise, by mingling the claims of body and soul in the manner of
The Extasie. For Donne held that love "though it be
directed upon the minde, doth inhere in the body, and
find piety entertainment there." [2] Of the compromise
which enabled him to reconcile his nature to the rule
of Holy Orders, we catch many hints in *The Litanie*,
which is a valuable testament to the conclusions we
read in his life:

1. *Letters* (1910), p. 119.   2. *Ibid.*, p. 104.

From being anxious, or secure,
Dead clods of sadnesse, or light squibs of mirth,
　From thinking, that great courts immure
All, or no happinesse, or that this earth
　　Is only for our prison fram'd,
　　Or that thou art covetous
To them whom thou lovest, or that they are maim'd
From reaching this worlds sweet, who seek thee thus,
With all their might, Good Lord deliver us.[1]

When Donne finally bent his head to the yoke, he must have been in this frame of mind. His love for Anne More had taught him the only way to a harmony of soul that lay open to such a nature, the way of self-effacement; this is the way he took when he embraced Holy Orders.[2] When she died, the former discord, only resolved in his love for her, asserted its old malignancy in the troubled accents of the *Holy Sonnets*, where he is once more terribly alone with himself.

The most puzzling collision in Donne's mind is not that between the old and the new learning, but rather that between the spirit of the Renascence and the spirit of the Reformation. His early travels had nurtured him in the spirit of the Renascence in Latin countries, especially in the pagan sensuality of a Catullus; and yet, however considerable this foreign influence may have been, it did not alter the intense individuality of his genius. Even in his early years the study of divinity had satisfied a certain craving of his mind. During

1. Written about 1609. See *Letters* (1910), no. xii, where the story of the new *Litanie* and the recent *Biathanatos* is told.
2. See *Holy Sonnets*, no. xvii, for an intimate revelation of mind.

the time of his greatest distress, scepticism was creeping into England with Montaigne; I have already
shown how this entered into his thought in those
years. It gave a permanent cast to his thinking, but
it had been definitely stated in his verse as early as
the *Third Satire*, between 1594 and 1597:

> doubt wisely; in strange way
> To stand inquiring right, is not to stray;
> To sleepe, or runne wrong, is.[1]

So the virus was early in his blood. With such a mind
Donne, while in Paris with Sir Robert Drury, saw and
believed the vision of his dear wife passing twice by
him through the room, with her hair hanging about
her shoulders, and a dead child in her arms. It is just
such a mind, so strangely compounded of mysticism
and logic, that we find everywhere in his life and in
the rapid alteration of feeling in his poetry.

If he has any consistent philosophy, it is that of the
arch-sceptic of the time, Montaigne: it is learning how
to die — a view that Montaigne took from Cicero.
Donne early thought of death and was possessed by
an over-earnest desire of the next life. He had the
same desire when he went with the tide, and he was
often too "well content to be nothing — that is,
dead." His contemplation of suicide in *Biathanatos*
is more than anything else a purgation of the mind, a
rationalization of this desire. Such purgation was an
imperative need of his mind, as the composition of
hymns and devotions while in the agony of the sick-

1. Grierson, *op. cit.*, i, 157.

bed proves, or as these lines from *The triple Foole* confess:

> I thought, if I could draw my paines,
> Through Rimes vexation, I should them allay,
> Griefe brought to numbers cannot be so fierce,
> For, he tames it, that fetters it in verse.

Even within the Church the effort to still his beating mind and tame his naked, thinking heart must have been tremendous. To make matters worse, his heart never forgot its hydroptic youth, and his mind, so eager for the light of reason, had to be subdued to faith in the Augustinian doctrine of grace.

He was enamored of death as of a supernatural mistress who both fascinated and terrified him; for the mystical passions which she aroused in him, he clothed her in a dress of logic: it was his necessary gift. In no English poet has death lent such a background of mystery and terror to a mode of thinking and feeling. Even when he writes an epithalamion he cannot banish the thought of death:

> Leave, leave, faire Bride, your solitary bed,
>   No more shall you returne to it alone,
> It nourseth sadnesse, and your bodies print,
> Like to a grave, the yielding downe doth dint.[1]

In his magnificent last *Death's Duell* a deep note of the old discord between body and soul comes out in the poet's fear of the carnal corruption of the grave. His final discipline in learning how to die came with

1. *Epithalamion made at Lincolnes Inne*, Grierson, *op. cit.*, i, 141.

his shroud; he met it with the resolution, a little an-
guished I think, of the *Hymne to God the Father*:

> I have a sinne of feare, that when I have spunne
> My last thred, I shall perish on the shore;
> But sweare by thy selfe, that at my death thy sonne
> Shall shine as he shines now, and heretofore;
> And, having done that, Thou haste done,
> I feare no more.

The terrific puns in this divine verse show how the
whole Donne was present in every thought and every
feeling. This terminated a discipline of the spirit as
significant as that of Baudelaire, but more successful,
except in the mastery of numbers, which suffered
from the violence of the struggle.

Such was the nature of the poet for whom I have
tried to give those greater facts which mould and
color all the artist's work. Only an analysis of the
poetry itself will make this relationship cogent; will
show us, for instance, why the unified sensibility of
Donne made the discordant claims of body and soul,
Court and Church, so distressing. Immensely valuable as an explorer of the soul and as a study in the
discipline of the spirit, Donne is likewise profoundly
significant in the history of English verse. And yet
as a poet he was early consigned to the dust of yes-
terday.

NOTE. Mr. F. P. Wilson has found evidence to show that Donne was
probably born in 1572, and that his patrimony was about a fourth of
Walton's figure. On these points I have allowed Walton's *Life* to stand
uncorrected.

II. THE NATURE OF THE DONNE TRADITION

:xxxxxxxxxxxxxxxxxxxxxxxxxxxxxxxxxxxxxxxxxxxxxxxxxxxxxxx:

IT IS now more than three hundred years since Ben Jonson told Drummond of Hawthornden "that Done himself, for not being understood would perish." It is nearly half that time since Dr. Johnson, speaking of those he was the first to call the Metaphysical poets, declared that "these writers will, without great wrong, lose their right to the name of poets." Though he made this prophecy subject to the validity of Aristotle, we may be sure that he was in no doubt of the issue.

Yet the times have never been riper for the understanding of Donne than in our own day, if we may judge from the studies which scholars have devoted to him since Grierson's great edition. These studies include such unusual items as the handsome bibliography by Geoffrey Keynes, the esoteric French dissertation by Miss Ramsay, and the fine Italian study by Mario Praz. Nor are these the only signs of a very live interest in Donne at the present time. In these later days — in fact, since Browning — Donne has again become a very living influence with our poets. This phenomenon has begun to attract the attention of the critics, and of late it has even penetrated to the weekly press.[1]

1. See "Two Elements in Poetry" by John Gould Fletcher in the *Saturday Review of Literature*, 27 August, 1927, p. 66.

Despite such interest, the place of the Donne tradition in the current of English poetry has yet to be adequately defined in our literary history. Since Dr. Johnson wrote the judgment which has stuck,[1] although the chief elements in his indictment are as old as Dryden,[2] — whose reasons to condemn are not ours, — it is to Johnson that we must return in any revaluation of Donne. The influence of Donne in his own century, and in subsequent centuries, will show that he belongs in the direct current of English poetry and not in one of its eccentric eddies. But only the other day Professor Legouis thrust Donne back into limbo with these words: "John Donne ... is perhaps the most singular of English poets. His verses offer examples of everything castigated by classical writers as bad taste and eccentricity, all pushed to such an extreme that the critic's head swims as he condemns." [3] And Professor Legouis is not alone in this opinion.

With such a view before us, we need to arrive at a clear analysis of the nature of Donne's poetry before we can consider it as the beginning of a poetic tradition. Dr. Johnson tried to describe Donne's poetry by its defects, and criticism down to Courthope has tended to follow this path. Metaphysical wit and the conceit get a large share of this condemnatory criticism, which fails to account for the power of Donne and his growing vogue with lovers of poetry.

1. *Lives of the English Poets: Cowley.*
2. See *Discourse concerning Satire* and Dedication to *Eleonora.*
3. *History of English Literature* (650–1660), p. 215.

Modern critics, such as Gosse, Grierson, and Praz, are more likely to be struck by the intellectual intensity of Donne, the marriage of reason and passion, the embrace of Apollo and Dionysus. To Gosse this intellectual intensity is "the great gift which Donne passed down to his disciples";[1] to Grierson it is a "peculiar blend of passion and thought,"[2] and the greatest achievement of the Metaphysical poets; to T. S. Eliot it is a "direct sensuous apprehension of thought, or a recreation of thought into feeling."[3] This quality will appear in a typical passage from Donne, this from *The Extasie*:

> As our blood labours to beget
>   Spirits, as like soules as it can,
> Because such fingers need to knit
>   That subtile knot, which makes us man:
> So must pure lovers soules descend
>   T'affections, and to faculties,
> Which sense may reach and apprehend,
>   Else a great Prince in prison lies.
> To' our bodies turne wee then, that so
>   Weake men on love reveal'd may looke;
> Loves mysteries in soules doe grow,
>   But yet the body is his booke.

Here a Dionysian ecstasy is supported by the coolest reason, and neither feeling nor thought can be separated from its sensuous embodiment. This is no poetizing of thought, but thought in the flesh of sensuous and emotional perception, or mind expressing itself

1. *More Books on the Table:* "Metaphysical Poetry," p. 311.
2. Introduction to *Metaphysical Poetry*, p. xvi.
3. *Homage to John Dryden*, p. 29.

in the book of the body.[1] Some idea of the distinction
I am trying to make with respect to Donne's thinking may be had by a reference to Keats. In one of his
letters Keats says, "Axioms in philosophy are not
axioms till they are proved upon our pulses."[2] Just
so, thoughts were not thoughts for Donne till they
were proved upon his pulses, not set down with ac-
companiments on the pulses as they are in Tennyson.[3] This remark of Keats, which throws new light
on his desire for a life of sensations rather than of
thoughts, describes Donne's natural way of appre-
hending thought. Mr. J. M. Murry's claim that it is
impossible to isolate the faculties of Keats's mind is
even truer of Donne's.

This intellectual intensity derives its peculiar
power from the unified sensibility which makes it impossible to isolate the faculties of Donne. As T. S.
Eliot has said, "The range of his feeling was great,
but no more remarkable than its unity. He was altogether present in every thought and every feeling."[4] Perhaps nothing is more remarkable than the
unity of feeling which runs through the variety of his
love songs, unity in the sense that every mood under
which he groups the elements of love seems implicit
in the mood which dominates any given poem. *The
Flea* and *The Extasie* involve similar elements, the
same real theme and conclusion, but their moods

1. See Eliot's idea that Donne ends "a period when the intellect was
immediately at the tips of the senses." *The Sacred Wood*, p. 117.
2. Letter to Reynolds, 3 May, 1818.
3. Particularly in such poems as *Locksley Hall*.
4. "John Donne," *Nation and Athenaeum*, 9 June, 1923.

seem poles apart: and yet we know how easily in
Donne one may change to the other, and how one
philosophy is the postulate of both moods. His unified sensibility makes his images the very body of his
thought, not something added to it:

> No use of lanthornes; and in one place lay
> Feathers and dust, to day and yesterday.
> Earths hollownesses, which the worlds lungs are,
> Have no more winde then the upper valt of aire.
> We can nor lost friends, nor sought foes recover,
> But meteorlike, save that wee move not, hover.
> Onely the Calenture together drawes
> Deare friends, which meet dead in great fishes jawes.[1]

The first two lines are those Ben Jonson so much admired. This sensuous thinking is both described and
embodied in a passage in the *Second Anniversarie*:

> When wilt thou shake off this Pedantery,
> Of being taught by sense, and Fantasie? . . .
> Thou shalt not peepe through lattices of eyes,
> Nor heare through Labyrinths of eares, nor learne
> By circuit, or collections to discerne.[2]

And yet this is the way Donne was always thinking;
what he wrote of Elizabeth Drury is peculiarly true
of him: his body thought.[3] This trait he shares with
Shakspere and Chapman, but not with Ben Jonson,

1. *The Calme*, Grierson, *Donne's Poetical Works*, i, 178.
2. Grierson, *op. cit.*, i, 259–260.
3. See *Letters* (1910), no. xxv, where he says that "we consist of
three parts, a Soul, and Body, and Minde: which I call those thoughts
and affections and passions, which neither soul nor body hath alone, but
have been begotten by their communication, as Musique results out of
our breath and a Cornet."

who was much more conscious of the dualism of thought and sense. Comparison of *The Second Anniversarie* with *In Memoriam* or *Rabbi Ben Ezra* will show that the nineteenth-century poets have lost this quality, that they think and feel by starts, that their images are not the very body of their thought.[1] Much as this sensuous thinking may seem an essential of all poetry, there has been little of it and its source, a unified sensibility, in English poetry since the seventeenth century. Keats was working toward it in his second *Hyperion*.

The rule of wit which has often been singled out as the chief characteristic of Donne is closely related to his use of the conceit and of surprise. For Courthope the heading, "School of Metaphysical Wit," is enough to dispose of Donne. Dr. Johnson began the difficult task of defining this wit, and we cannot do better than to begin, and perhaps to end, with his definition. He describes it "as a kind of *discordia concors*; a combination of dissimilar images, or discovery of occult resemblances in things apparently unlike." He adds: "Of wit, thus defined, they have more than enough. The most heterogeneous ideas are yoked by violence together."[2] As an indictment the force of this statement lies in the words *yoked* and *violence*: *yoked* denies the union necessary to the good poetic image, and *violence* implies an effect which the mind will not accept. As a definition

1. See T. S. Eliot, *Homage to John Dryden*, pp. 30–31, for an excellent statement of this difference. Especially in this part of my work I owe much to his brilliant analysis.
2. *Lives of the Poets: Cowley* (World's Classics), i, 14.

of wit it does not differ from a description of the operation of the poetic mind, except in the degree of compulsion exerted by that mind. As an indictment this
analysis applies to all poetry which errs in the respects named, and no more to so-called Metaphysical
poetry than the frequency of such errors justifies,
which its enemies will think often enough. My point
is that the charge can be made against poetry other
than the Metaphysical, while the definition can be
applied to the common operation of the poetic mind.

Dr. Johnson goes on to deny to this wit the achievement of the pathetic and the sublime, a judgment so
unfair that it can be refuted by just two lines from
Donne:

> So, so break off this last lamenting kiss.[1]

>   so long,
> As till Gods great *Venite* change the song.[2]

Even in another hand this wit could achieve an emotional effect not often met; observe the effect of terror in these lines, especially in the figure, from *The
Exequy* of Donne's disciple, Bishop King:

> But heark! My Pulse like a soft Drum
> Beats my approach, tells Thee I come;
> And slow howere my marches be,
> I shall at last sit down by Thee.

These lines reveal typical Metaphysical wit and abilities denied to it, but they have the power and produce the effects which belong to all true poetry. Al-

1. *The Expiration*, Grierson, *op. cit.*, i, 68.
2. *The Second Anniversarie, ibid.*, p. 252.

though Dr. Johnson's charge that wit was used to show the author's ingenuity and learning is too often true, especially of Donne's imitators, such faults are faults which have appeared wherever the conceit has appeared; and they should be reprimanded by the general standards of English poetry, not accepted as the defective virtues of the Metaphysical school.

If we accept Dr. Johnson's definition of wit as applicable to more than the school for which he coined it, we must still admit many of the particular charges which he makes, though we may differ from him in our judgment of their offensiveness. But first of all we should observe that this wit, or *discordia concors*, may produce an intellectual effect or an imaginative effect. In one case it pleases by its mental ingenuity, and in another by its imaginative shock; in other words, it may be what we call witty, or it may be profoundly moving: in *The Flea* it is witty, in *A Valediction: forbidding mourning* it is moving. These two possible effects of wit relate to one of the particular charges of Johnson, that the Metaphysical poets "lay on the watch for novelty." Criticism has long ago set down their excesses in this direction, but it has failed properly to recognize this watch for novelty as a search for one of the essentials of all poetry — surprise.[1] Both Johnson, in his discussion of wit, and Coleridge, in his account of poetry,[2] recognize the value of surprise. Now Donne achieved surprise

1. Of course it is the surprise that wears, the surprise that accompanies the imaginative shock and does not vanish at the second reading.
2. *Biographia Literaria*, chap. 14.

chiefly through wit, appealing both to intellect and
to imagination; and his principal means of getting
this surprise was the conceit. The close relation of
these three things in Donne, wit, surprise, conceit,
accounts for the nature of his immediate influence
and reputation in the seventeenth century. But the
poetic hazards of the conceit, which often confused
his early imitators, should not be allowed to obscure
the genuine worth of these elements to poetry in
general.

How Donne employed wit for both intellectual and
imaginative surprise may be shown in a few illustra-
tions:

When my grave is broke up againe
Some second ghest to entertaine,[1]

For if the sinewie thread my braine lets fall
        Through every part,
Can tye those parts, and make mee one of all;[2]

I could eclipse and cloud them with a winke,
But that I would not lose her sight so long:[3]

Hope not for minde in women; at their best
Sweetnesse and wit, they'are but *Mummy*, possest.[4]

                O more then Moone,
Draw not up seas to drowne me in thy spheare,
Weepe me not dead, in thine armes, but forbeare
To teach the sea, what it may doe too soone.[5]

1. *The Relique*, Grierson, *op. cit.*, i, 62.
2. *The Funerall*, *ibid.*, p. 58.
3. *Sunne Rising*, *ibid.*, p. 11.
4. *Loves Alchymie*, *ibid.*, p. 40.
5. *A Valediction: of weeping*, *ibid.*, p. 39.

In these examples the contrast of single words, the sudden juxtaposition of ideas, or the compulsion of a neutral term into a powerful metaphorical relation is enough to give us a witty or imaginative shock. Such an example as "O more then Moone" is both ingenious and imaginative, a combination that Donne and his followers often achieved with astonishing and beautiful results. It is in such combination that the conceit attains to high poetic value; the idea and figure become one, and we have Donne's *Valediction*, King's *Exequy*, Herbert's *Pulley*, or Marvell's *Coy Mistress*. Donne's use of the compasses may have been proposed by ingenuity, but it is justified by imagination, as any figure must be to be successful. Poems like these defeat the critics who have condemned the conceit out of hand for having that touch of the self-conscious which, according to Croce, deprives art of its essential nature; for these poems are moving and sincere. The assertion [1] that the deeper the emotion the simpler must be its figurative expression here breaks down, and the fact seems to be that only the force of emotion limits the complexity of the figures which it can carry. Given this emotional lift, the conceit, though self-conscious, satisfies the exposition of imagination given by Coleridge.[2] In such poems as those named the conceit is a larger element of surprise and the chief instrument of wit. Since it was the most imitable trait of Donne's verse, it was the most imitated and the chief item in his

---

1. See Society for Pure English Tract, No. XI: *Metaphor*, part i, by E. B.   2. *Op. cit.*, chap. 14.

reputation as a wit. As such it demands a clear definition of its very elusive qualities.

What is the peculiar nature of the Donne conceit? We have seen its close relation to wit and poetic surprise; we may find a list of minatory examples in Johnson's essay on Cowley; but where are we to find its essence? We may think of it as the shock troop which Donne used in his revolt against Petrarchianism and in his re-creation of the lyric expression of personal experience; we may think of it as the natural expression of an ingenious mind; or we may think of it as an Elizabethan device which he turned to account as an instrument of wit and poetic surprise.

Before we attempt an answer, however, we ought to look a little more squarely at the wit we have been considering. Is this wit merely the most heterogeneous ideas yoked by violence together? Dr. Johnson himself has given us the germ of an answer: he says, "Their attempts were always analytic; they broke every image into fragments." [1] Now the tool of analysis is reason; and the rule of reason appeared in English poetry with Ben Jonson and John Donne, whose reason, though dialectical, was doubtless the ground for mutual respect between him and Jonson. At any rate, the rational basis of wit is felt in all Metaphysical poetry. T. S. Eliot has defined this wit as "a tough reasonableness beneath the slight lyric grace." [2] One is always conscious of this tough reasonableness in the evolution of Donne's conceits and even of his poems. Breaking images into fragments

1. *Op. cit.*, i, 15.   2. *Homage to John Dryden*, p. 35.

demands the rational perception of relations. When this perception is adroit and unemotional it tickles our fancy, and we call it witty; when it is profound and emotional it stirs our sensibility, and we call it imaginative. In either case there is a rational basis in the discovery of resemblances and in their development as a poem. Another distinctive mark of Donne's wit is the range of material from which he permitted himself to draw in his perception of analogies; this relates to what he knew. A third mark is the imaginative distance between the things he united, sometimes merely yoked, into an image; this also is related to the breadth of his knowledge. All three marks distinguish his use of the conceit.

Donne really uses two sorts of conceit. One is what we may call the expanded conceit, which is the exposition of an extended comparison; the other is the condensed conceit, which is a telescoped image that develops the thought by rapid association or sudden contrast. *A Valediction*, with its compasses, is a good example of the expanded conceit; and *The Extasie* shows an electric use of the condensed conceit, whose most remarkable employment in sudden contrast appears in the second line of this passage:

> And he that digs it, spies
> A bracelet of bright haire about the bone,
> Will he not let' us alone,
> And thinke that there a loving couple lies.[1]

The expanded conceit is successful when the idea and figure become one, and the condensed conceit

1. *The Relique*, Grierson, *op. cit.*, i, 62.

when the image is the very body of the thought. Thus we see the close relation of the conceit to the sensuous thinking of Donne which I have already described. The conceit, playing like a shuttle between his mind and the world, wove the fabric of his thought, and gave the pattern in which he united his most disparate knowledge and experience into an image witty or imaginative, novel or compelling, but always rising from a tough reasonableness and often attaining startling insight, with moments of breathtaking beauty. In short, the conceit, with its wit and surprise and bias of reason, suited his mind, his many-sided interests, and his poetic nature. Grierson's belief [1] that shock, surprise, and contradiction in evolution, language, and imagery constitute the essence of Donne's poetry bears witness to the importance of the conceit in the relation we have been discussing. From analysis Donne's conceits achieve synthesis.

The laboratory of this synthesis is the "naked, thinking heart" of Donne, where the conceit becomes a microscope held over pulsing emotions. Here, looking more sharply, we may discover how Donne, like Paul Valéry, "chained an analysis to an ecstasy" and gave us the impassioned geometry of his verse. To discover the secret of this analytic art, we need to look at the conceit from another angle, to see it as a special type of metaphor, which Mr. Henry W. Wells has called "the Radical image." [2] "In Radical im-

1. See his review of Praz's study of Donne, *Review of English Studies*, vol. ii, no. 8, p. 467.
2. See chap. on "The Radical Image" in his *Poetic Imagery*.

agery the minor term is itself of little imaginative
value but the metaphorical relation is powerful,"
says Mr. Wells, and adds, "The minor term in a Radical image is significant metaphorically only at a single, narrow point of contact. Elsewhere it is incon-
gruous." Looking at Donne's conceit from this point
of view, we see how a poetically neutral idea like the
compasses in *A Valediction: forbidding mourning* can
be brought into a powerful metaphorical relation by
an imaginative act that is also analytical. This view
is in agreement with Dr. Johnson's definition of wit.
To illustrate the "single, narrow point of contact," as
well as the forcible neutralization of the minor term
which Donne practised, one could scarcely find a better or more typical example than this image from
the *First Anniversary*:

> But as some Serpents poyson hurteth not,
> Except it be from the live Serpent shot,
> So doth her vertue need her here, to fit
> That unto us; shee working more than it.[1]

A scientific point of view here neutralizes the "Serpents
poyson" and insures the desired effect. Mr. Wells
shows how Radical figures clarify obscure ideas, give
a vivid form to familiar ones, and become almost a
necessity to the expression of mystical experience.
One can but agree with him that the conceit, or what
he calls the Radical image, is an essential medium of
expression for Donne's introspective analysis.

How much the conceit or the Radical image is the
very body of his thought, how nearly inexpressible

1. Grierson, *op. cit.*, i, 243.

that thought is without this structural decoration, appears nowhere better than in an image of death from the *Second Anniversarie*:

> And thinke that, but unbinding of a packe,
> To take one precious thing, thy soule from thence.[1]

Here we have a fine example, and Donne is full of like examples, of analytic thought achieving poetic synthesis. We shall not be wrong if we conclude that the conceit is one of the principal means by which Donne chained analysis to ecstasy; never, we remember, more characteristically than in the poem called *The Extasie*. The nature of the minor term in his Radical image made the ugly and trivial available for poetry, and opened a mine of realistic possibilities which his contemporaries too often were unable to fuse into a compelling metaphorical relation. In Donne and in the drama of his time, thought entered into imaginative content chiefly through this minor term, which thereafter did yeoman's service for the Metaphysical poets.

Of even more importance is the analytic nature of Donne's poetry apart from his use of the conceit. Sir Edmund Gosse has said that perhaps we get nearest to the secret of the Metaphysical poets "when we say that their object was an application of the psychological method to the passions."[2] Dr. Johnson would admit that they dissected a sunbeam with a prism, but never the passions, though their attempts were always analytic. Modern critical opinion, however, is certainly nearer to Gosse; for much of Donne's

---

1. *Donne's Poetical Works*, i, 254.   2. *Ibid.*, p. 309.

present fascination, as well as his extraordinary originality, is "his fidelity to emotion as he finds it; his
recognition of the complexity of feeling and its rapid
alterations and antitheses."[1]   Most of the psychological subtlety we find in Browning, especially in regard to love, is already in Donne, from whom Browning certainly drew much of his philosophy of body
and soul. Sidney had told the poet to look in his
heart and write, but in a comprehensive and profound way no one but Shakspere did till Donne.
But then, as T. S. Eliot remarks, Donne "looked
into a good deal more than the heart";[2] he looked
into the cerebral cortex, the nervous system, and the
physical reflexes. It is because he is expressing the
whole tangle of his feelings that his poetry has so
much psychological realism. Indeed he told his own
age that

> Love 's not so pure, and abstract, as they use
> To say, which have no Mistresse but their Muse.

After the Petrarchian and pastoral superficialities of
the Elizabethan lyric, Donne is shocking in his curious exploration of the soul.

How analysis becomes the very genius of his conceit and of his psychological method has been suggested, but little has been said of its relation to the
evolution of his thought. Writing of the Metaphysical strain in Donne, Mario Praz lays chief stress on

1. Eliot, "John Donne," *Nation and Athenaeum*, 9 June, 1923.
2. *Homage to John Dryden*, p. 33. Writing to Sir Henry Wotton,
Donne says, "You (I think) and I am much of one sect in the Philosophy
of love; which though it be directed upon the minde, doth inhere in the
body, and find piety entertainment there." *Letters* (1910), p. 104.

the curious contrast of direct expressions and ratiocinative processes.[1] After analyzing some of his
verse, Praz concludes that many of his poems "degenerate into fatiguing and involved labyrinths of
thought."[2] According to Mr. Praz, the opening lines
of *Loves Deitie*,

> I long to talke with some old lovers ghost
>   Who dyed before the god of Love was borne,

prepare us, by their musical incantation, for a poem
like Villon's *Dames du temps jadis*; whereas we get an
argument on unrequited love.[3] This position I, for
one, cannot accept. The words *talke* and *lovers ghost*
prepare us not so much for a recital of beautiful dead
ladies as for some quest of amatory knowledge, which
may resort, in true Donne fashion, to thought; and
the second line prepares for the answer which might
have come before the reign of Cupid. Surely the
wistful mood and meditative music of the opening
are as appropriate for unrequited love as for a ballad
of beautiful ladies! And if the poet happens to be
Donne, one of mercurial mood, we may expect the
whole tangle of his feelings and more variety in the
unity of the poem. The development is argumentative and analytic in characteristic fashion, but it
does not degenerate into fatiguing and involved labyrinths of thought, however it may seem to drop in
lyric pitch. Not a little of this drop is due to the fact
that the voice of reason is drowned in the lyric cry of
the first lines until we see their purport in those which

1. *Secentismo e Marinismo in Inghilterra*, pp. 93 ff.
2. *Ibid.*, p. 102.   3. *Ibid.*, pp. 95 ff.

follow. And it must be remembered that Donne made use of arresting openings after the fashion of the modern short story: sometimes he startled with brusque directness and sometimes with magnificence. Finally, it is useless to complain that Donne is not Campion or Villon, and to judge him as if he were.

The analytic and logical development of Donne's poetry is probably at bottom the reason for the assertion that he frequently wrote magnificent passages, especially beginnings, but few whole poems. Many feel that his poems degenerate as Praz has described. This is a serious charge, but I believe that its truth has been greatly exaggerated. Suppose we take *The Autumnall* for example. It has been esteemed as a magnificent beginning, with a falling away of lyric expression; it begins with the lines,

> No *Spring*, nor *Summer* Beauty hath such grace,
> As I have seen in one *Autumnall* face.

Since my space is limited, I cannot quote the whole poem, which the reader is invited to examine; but I can illustrate the quality of lyric expression which follows this magnificent beginning. Let me quote a line or two at intervals, and then the final lines of the poem:

> Here, where still *Evening* is; not *noone*, nor *night*;
> .   .   .   .
> *Age* must be lovelyest at the latest day.
> .   .   .   .
> Not panting after growing beauties, so,
> I shall ebbe out with them, who home-ward goe.

These lines adumbrate the thought of the poem, its
lucid evolution, continuity of mood, color of realism,
and recurring lyric reach. Is it too much to say that
here is little, if any, falling away in lyric expression?
I will admit a blemish or so, but I fail to see why *The
Autumnall* is not a whole poem rather than merely a
magnificent beginning, and a poem whose logical and
esthetic conclusion is worthy of its beginning.

But let me quote another much praised beginning,
an additional line or so, and then the conclusion.
Let it be from *The good-morrow*, which I must ask my
reader to recall as a whole:

> I Wonder by my troth, what thou, and I
> Did, till we lov'd? were we not wean'd till then?
> . . . .
>
> For love, all love of other sights controules,
> And makes one little roome, an every where.
> . . . .
>
> If our two loves be one, or, thou and I
> Love so alike, that none doe slacken, none can die.

Here again I fail to see the great degeneracy of lyric
expression, and neither in this poem nor in *The Autumnall* can I find more difficulty than a tough reasonableness beneath the lyric grace; certainly there is
no fatiguing labyrinth of thought. Furthermore,
none of these charges can be proved against such
poems as *The Relique*, *The Dreame*, *The Funerall*, and
even *The Extasie*, or *Lovers infinitenesse*; none save
the tough reasonableness which is ever the mark of
Donne and which permits his most daring imagina-

tive leaps. We should guard against admitting too
many of his poems into the category described by
Praz, for his logical development of thought makes
his poems hold together with something more than
the Jonsonian sense of form; it is a peculiarity of
his lyric form which may sometimes be too tough for
his song, but which, nevertheless, is something per-
manently valuable for English poetry. One might
say of Donne, as Conrad has said of Proust, that "his
is a creative art absolutely based on analysis. It is
really more than that. He is a writer who has pushed
analysis to the point when it becomes creative."
But no matter how analytic Donne may be, he puts
his material together again in a new unity based on
a logical substructure and defined by a dominant
mood.

I wonder how many of those who read "*Sweetest
love, I do not goe*" realize the subtle logic from which
its crystal music flows. Even in this song Donne employs his argumentative evolution of thought while
he applies his analysis to leave-taking. Perhaps I
shall be pardoned a paraphrase of the thought of so
lovely a song for the sake of catching this side of his
lyric genius. Here is the lover's argument:

"Sweetest love, I do not goe because I tire of you or hope
for better love, but because I should learn to die, since once
I must, by taking leave of you. Last night the sun left,
and now has returned for no reason at all; so do not fear
for me, who take more reasons than he knew. How feeble
is man, who cannot prolong good fortune by a single hour,
but must always increase misfortune with his own strength!

When you grieve, you grieve my very self away; you cannot love me as you say, if you waste me whose best part is you. So do not anticipate any ill for me, lest destiny fulfil it; but think we have only gone to sleep; thus keeping one another alive, we shall never be parted."

This is a perfectly linked chain of thought, leading to a conclusion that is dependent on all that goes before, giving the music a kind of harmonic progression, and building our satisfaction in the lovely song on a basis of the hardest mathematics. Nothing is more characteristic of Donne than the way in which thought gives a mathematical basis to the music of his emotions. The crystalline logic of his poetry is comparable to the score of music, and to certain minds it gives a pleasure similar to that of reading a musical score as opposed to hearing it.

In *Lovers infinitenesse* a subtler logic leads to a subtler conclusion in the psychology of love, but the music carries it into our emotional understanding no less surely. That the method of analysis came into congenial and adroit hands with Donne is a matter of literary history; for ever since the time of Carew the critics have testified to his "universall monarchy of wit," and in later times to "the new psychological curiosity with which he writes of love and religion." [1] Only Shakspere among Elizabethan song-writers and sonneteers can show anything like the depth and range of feeling and psychological perception that we find in Donne.

When we approach the technical side of Donne's

1. Grierson, Introduction to *Metaphysical Poetry*, p. xiv.

verse, we come upon another paradox that has be-
wildered, enraged, or enchanted posterity. Ben Jonson, friend and admirer of Donne, raised the first
dissenting voice when he declared to Drummond that
"Done, for not keeping of accent, deserved hanging";
and he added confusion to condemnation when he asserted that Donne was "the first poet in the world in
some things." The charge of not keeping accent applies least to the lyrics and most to the satires; the
miscellaneous poems occupy a middle ground. The
metrical felicity of the lyrics, though not easy, makes
the most violent contrast with the cacophony of the
satires, bringing to a focus the prosodic puzzle of
Donne. The satires may be explained by the Elizabethan notion, probably derived from the study of
Persius, that the rhythm of satire should be rough.
But the harsh or rugged quality of the rest of Donne's
verse has brought forth many theories designed to
explain away the mystery. Let me state several of
them so that the problem may come to us in better
perspective. Saintsbury sees in Donne's practice "a
rather irresponsible experiment"; [1] Fletcher Melton
discovers the key to the puzzle in his use of the same
sound now in *arsis* and now in *thesis*; [2] Grierson describes the secret as "the troubling of the regular fall
of the verse stresses by the intrusion of rhetorical
stress on syllables which the metrical pattern leaves
unstressed, and, secondly, an echoing and reëchoing
of similar sounds parallel to his fondness for resem-

1. *History of English Prosody*, ii, 165.
2. *The Rhetoric of John Donne's Verse*, chap. 10.

blances in thoughts and things apparently the most
remote from one another"; [1] Praz believes that, except for the satires, Donne's poetry was nearly always written on the rhythmical basis of the stanza
rather than of the single verse;[2] while Eliot observes
that English verse at the beginning of the seventeenth century reveals the "constant evasion and
recognition of regularity." [3] All of these theories
have their truth, and each may at some moment
seem the vade-mecum to this disturbing verse; but
there may be a larger factor which accounts for these
items and yet escapes our notice.

I mean simply the astringent effect of intellect on
the facility of verse. A mind so original and so personal as Donne's is bound to shape its language signifi-
cantly; indeed, it is from his language that we deduce
these adjectives. Now intellect and psychological
integrity stamp his verse, and constantly remind us
that meaning was paramount with him. Although
there is little doubt of the revolt and experiment in
Donne, these facts themselves find their sufficient
cause in the character of his mind. Since verse places
its accents on the sounds and not on the sense, and
since intellect places its accents on the sense and not
on the sounds, we need not be surprised that his
poetry is found to serve two masters, with less than
the usual chance of reconciliation. On the rare occasions when sound and sense coincide in a compelling

1. Introduction to *Metaphysical Poetry*, p. xxiv.
2. *Op. cit.*, pp. 138 ff.
3. "Reflections on Vers Libre," *New Statesman*, 3 March, 1917.

emotion, he gives us those things for which Jonson declared him the first poet in the world; on the more common occasions when sound is sacrificed a little to sense, he frequently gives us astounding things; but when, as in the satires, sound is sacrificed almost altogether to sense, he gives us the jarring monstrosities which even his admirers cannot quite condone. Coupled with his paradoxical and audacious spirit, it is intellect, the source of his famous wit, that produces the astringent effect which draws to his verse the epithets of harsh and rugged; this astringency was part of the natural response of his mind to the even fatal facility of Spenserianism. It is a result of the reassertion of subject-matter in poetry. Only one thing could release this astringency and carry his thought to marvellous music, and that was the compelling emotion which gives us the finest of his love songs and divine poems.

Those who are sceptical may recall the well-known case of Shakspere in his last plays. The packed verse of these plays, with its increasing obscurity and tendency to depart from the iambic pentameter norm, is a clear case of the disturbing influence of growing complexity of thought. The more Shakspere approaches the density of Donne the more irregular and difficult he becomes. Parallel, too, is the complexity of sentence structure in the effort to be faithful to thought and feeling. Even in the couplet Donne uses the run-on line which Shakspere uses increasingly in blank verse. In short, the growing presence of intellect in Shakspere's verse brings irregularity, density, and more difficult syntax; or similar phenomena, however different in degree, to those we find in Donne.

While one may say that if Donne's intellect rebelled against the discipline of verse, the less poet he; one cannot say quite the same thing of Shakspere. However, in one remarkable way verse triumphed over the natural astringency of Donne's mind: that is in his use of the song where the sonnet would have been more natural. His passionate argumentative evolution of thought seems by its very nature to call for the meditative movement of the sonnet; but it actually comes to us, in its most enthralling form, in the winged movement of the song. While the song is less suited to his intellect, it gives a more electric quality to his passionate intensity and a more dazzling effect to his leaping and soaring imagination; and we must remember that, unruly as his intellect was, his passion and imagination were imperious in their demands. His thought is thus given wings; but his imagination does not rush pell-mell through its song, for it obeys the compelling mathematics of the argument and, with all its Dionysian intensity, reaches the resolution of a logical progression. His use of the song brings us back to the realization how impossible it is to isolate his faculties.

With this relation of Donne's verse to his mind, I return to an analysis of the peculiarities of the verse itself. Certain devices that serve to emphasize his paradox and meaning may be discovered in his verse; they may be taken as the conscious stylistic effects of a significant mind embodying itself in verse. One

such device Mr. Melton has found in the alternate
length and shortness of the same syllable, but I am
sure this is not so much the key to a new prosody as
it is a means of rousing the reader to the meaning of
the verse. Associated with this is the echoing of similar sounds throughout a passage. This repetition,
acting as a subtle variation of the refrain in poetry,
is both a means of emphasis and a means of creating
and sustaining a mood. Perhaps no line in Donne
could be a more pregnant text than

When thou knew'st what I dreamt, when thou knew'st
   when.[1]

Besides illustrating the devices I have mentioned,
this line shows the trick, common enough in Elizabethan dramatic verse, of beginning and ending a line
with the same sound; it also employs a colloquial turn
of phrasing in its use of *what* and *when*. This colloquial directness seems to be part of Donne's desire to
come as close to unconventional speech as possible,
a desire that doubtless sprang from the psychological
integrity of his mind and united with the paradoxical
nature of his thought.

  Although Donne is not elliptical as compared with
Browning, his sentence structure is often difficult and
the path of his thought is generally tortuous enough
to retard the natural flow of song, with the frequent
result that it gains in variety of music. This tortuous-
ness is no vice, but a fidelity to thought and feeling,
which often intrudes the rhythm of prose, accenting

1. *The Dreame*, Grierson, *Donne's Poetical Works*, i, 37.

the sense and not the sound, to the wrenching of the metrical rhythm and the startling of the mind. In this intrusion one is often reminded of the great rhetorical prose of the sermons which held their audience as if under a spell, and to the willing ear this reminder brings something of their massive music. It is only because the two rhythms coincide as often as they do that we get the soaring flight in difficult syntax. Donne, who was so great in self-knowledge, was not without such knowledge in regard to his own verse. Unless we take the following lines as conventional self-depreciation in an egoist who seldom felt such need, we may see in them an intimation of what I have been saying of the relation of his verse to his mind:

> Hast thee harsh verse, as fast as thy lame measure
>   Will give thee leave, to him, my pain and pleasure.
> I have given thee, and yet thou art too weake,
>   Feete, and a reasoning soule and tongue to speake.[1]

The reasoning soul of Donne's verse is, I believe, the principal source of its peculiarities, its glories and defects.

The conceit and its relation to Donne's wit, surprise, and way of thinking I have dealt with. A related problem is his use of language in general. Donne shocks the eye and ear with homely words and colloquial turns of phrase, and surprises with the contrast of learned words; but his staple vocabulary is characterized by the purity common to the seven-

1. "To M. T. W.," Grierson, *op. cit.*, i, 205.

teenth-century lyric. Such colloquial phrases as "For Godsake hold your tongue," "And wee said nothing, all the day," or "What I will say, I will not tell thee now," are numerous and typical; such homely words as *whining, rags, snorted,* and *itchy* mark even his love songs and divine poems; and learned words like *interinanimates, hydroptique, sublunary, trepidation* come into the music of his finest verse. Both his words and phrases vary from the simple and realistic to the fantastic and bizarre; his range is nearly compassed in

Get with child a mandrake roote.

And yet with all his strange mixture, he was master of a diction equally appropriate to his prose and verse. How important this is appears in the fact that the Metaphysicals were masters of the so-called "neutral style" in the seventeenth century.

The last phase of our analysis of Donne's poetry, and perhaps the first to impress a modern, is what Donne knew. Great as Milton was in learning, Donne was probably greater. In knowledge of the world they cannot be compared. Of all the explorers of the soul who come within the seventeenth century, Donne, and not Milton, deserves to stand nearest to Shakspere. And the two subjects in which he went deepest are those which try the understanding most — love and religion. From these twin sources in Donne flow significant currents in English poetry. Love poetry could never be quite the same after him, and religious verse that is also poetry descends from him.

Much of the nature of Donne's poetry is determined by what he knew. From the first his "hydroptic, immoderate thirst of human learning" carried
him into realms of knowledge and to interests rather
strange to the poetry of his time. Knowledge was a
passion with him: each adventure in learning must
have brought to him the frenzy of emotion which vis-
ited Keats upon opening Chapman's *Homer*. Ordinarily we think that knowledge in poetry has been
consciously vitalized by the poet; but with Donne
knowledge must have come living into his mind.
Mr. Murry has shown us the desire in young Keats
for knowledge received in an organic way; received,
as it were, alive into the mind.[1] Thus knowledge
came to Donne. Only this sensuous and emotional
apprehension of thought can account for the extraordinary mingling of what Donne learned from books
with what he learned from life — a mingling so spontaneous and natural that he finds all he knows
blended with his love and religion, and all he has
lived part and parcel of what he knows. Handling
ideas must have been almost a physical experience
to Donne, like caressing a shoulder or drinking wine.
No better proof of his unified sensibility could be
wanted than his *Anniversaries*, in which all his knowledge and all his experience are boldly mingled with
the character and death of Elizabeth Drury. The
suggestion of Dante's interfusion of the love of
woman and philosophy is not irrelevant here.[2]

1. See *Keats and Shakespeare*, chaps. 5 and 9.
2. Donne's knowledge of Dante appears in the fourth *Satire*, and in a
new letter (probably written by Donne to Wotton) which Simpson prints

Donne knew medieval scholasticism and theology, Dante and Rabelais, the New Learning, French and Italian and Spanish writers, the old physics, the new science of Copernicus, Galileo, and Bacon, and all that a profound psychological curiosity could gather from the experiences of an eventful life. His was one of those prodigious intellects which take all learning for their province, and one of those even rarer minds whose very thinking is poetical. How organic his thinking was appears again in the way in which the most abstract thought becomes a concrete or sentient thing in his poetry, acquires a sensuous habitation and a name, and is perceived by us through the lattices of eyes and the labyrinths of ears. The converse of this is that the concrete rises to the abstract in his eyes: a girl's cheeks become a thought, and he understands her by her sight. The profound unity of his sensibility is a condition of his amazing power to see resemblances, because the whole content of his mind, so various and extraordinary, is indissolubly one and incredibly connected. Associated with this power, the breadth of his knowledge accounts for the unusual imaginative distance between the elements of his images, and the depth of his knowledge accounts for those hyperboles which are not prompted by strong feeling or the spirit of paradox. This imaginative distance is what startles

(*Prose Works*, pp. 294–96). Dr. Simpson says: "Dante was little read in England during the sixteenth and seventeenth centuries, but Donne evidently studied him early in life, for we find an allusion in the fourth *Satire*: 'and a trance Like his, who dreamt he saw hell, did advance It selfe on mee' (Grierson, i, 164)."

us in his conceits and hyperboles, or makes us pause
to consider the figure in itself and thus provoke the
thought of self-consciousness. The nature of his
mind, with its unity in variety, also conditions his use
of images drawn from daily experience or scientific
knowledge, what Praz regards as "the too near at
hand and the too remote."[1] For Donne such restric-
tive terms did not exist; and the history of poetry,
with its changing incidental subject-matter, should
make us very chary of putting restrictions to poetic
imagery. Thus knowledge determined the nature of
his poetry.

Donne's subject-matter is mainly love and religion,
to which he brought immense learning, variety of
mood, and perhaps one dominating idea. His range
from sensual to mystical conceptions of love is an old
story, but less hackneyed is the relation of this range
to his religious thought. This relation involves another relation which is his dominant idea, the relation
of soul to body, or the theme of *The Extasie* and, in
one way or another, of so much of his poetry. In his
thought the body acquires a new worth which affects
both his conception of love and his religious feeling.
Nothing in his religious speculation is more striking
than his fear of death, which is peculiarly physical in
its dread of the "wormy circumstance" of dissolution.
Here in his thought we find a cold sensuality of the
grave which shows us that even his religious aspira-
tions could not shake off the dear enchantment of the
flesh, except by inverting it in physical repulsion.

1. *Op. cit.*, p. 121.

Just as he could ascend to the spiritual in his most physical conception of love, so in his religious thought he could not escape the implication of the body. For the body gives intense meaning to love and death, while death asks the most poignant questions of love and religion. This explains the great place given to death in his poetry, and in his sermons; culminating in those magnificent poems to death, the *Anniversaries*.

Those who see Donne's life sharply and rather inexplicably divided between profane and sacred love may find in this relation of body and soul some of the unity which they miss. For Donne, whether the priest of Apollo or of God, is always a poet of the same essential nature, and his ruling concept arises from his unified sensibility and corresponds to his organic way of thinking. In his life, as in his poems, all his moods are implicit in the mood dominant at a given moment: the priest is in the lover, and the lover in the priest; the divine poem is implicit in the love song, and the love song in the divine poem. A concrete example of this implication is the way in which the most typical mood of Donne, the mood of the charnel house, invades both his love songs and his divine poems. The importance and relevance of this mood to Donne should be apparent from the line of thought we have been following.

The quality in Donne which most appalls a lazy mind is his difficulty. This is not gratuitous; for a subtle and complex mind, devoted to the psychological realism which baffled his early imitators and often exercises his readers today, is responsible for the charge of obscurity which has been made against his poetry. Careful reading will not justify this charge, but will show that his difficulty is almost the opposite of obscurity: a question rather of too much light than of the lack of light. Swinburne has made a suggestive distinction between obscurity and difficulty in his essay on Chapman: "The difference between the two is the difference between smoke and lightning; and it is far more difficult to pitch the tone of your thought in harmony with that of a foggy thinker than with that of one whose thought is electric in its motion." He adds that the latter's "forked flashes of fancy and changing lights of thought move unerringly around one centre and strike straight in the end to one point." [1] A better description of Donne's poetry could scarcely be found, for his difficulty is precisely of the sort this electric thought entails. When his forked flashes of fancy strike, they stun us with the very energy of their motion, but as their light spreads out we see broad sweeps of thought which a moment before were buried in darkness. It is this quality of his verse that brings his admirers to a pitch of enthusiasm which loses itself in wonder. This flashing light of the mind and moments of massive and haunting music are enough to reduce the barriers which criticism has raised to keep the strange genius of Donne apart from the tradition of English poetry.

Before criticism began setting up these barriers with the opinions of Dryden, Donne had made his

1. *Contemporaries of Shakespeare*, p. 27.

own tradition in seventeenth-century poetry and Dryden had known its glamour. The Metaphysical school which descended from Donne gave the obvious character to his poetry that criticism has been prone to accept, but his disciples were conscious of more in the master than they were able to imitate. To Dr. Johnson their imitation appeared to carry them, and Donne, outside the direct current of English poetry, which for Johnson had well-defined banks. But what Donne meant to the Metaphysicals is much nearer to the nature his influence has taken in poetry since them, and much truer in its judgment of his worth to the English poetic tradition. Fortunately, we have an excellent criticism of his poetry made by a contemporary who was enough of his school to be sympathetic and enough of Ben Jonson's to know classical restraint: I refer to Carew's *Elegie upon the death of the Deane of Pauls, Dr. John Donne.* In this elegy we shall find what must have been a pretty general view of Donne expressed with more feeling than is usual in Carew.[1] Nothing could be more useful for our understanding of the Donne tradition as it arose.

Carew first laments that Donne's fire — both as Apollo's and the true God's priest — must be desired forever, and then describes his thinking as the heat and light that

> Did through the eye the melting heart distill;
> And the deepe knowledge of darke truths so teach,
> As sense might judge, what phansie could not reach.

1. See numerous echoes in *Elegies upon the Author*, Grierson.

Unless I mistake, this is exactly the sort of thinking I have been trying to point out in Donne: that sensuous embodiment of thought which came naturally from his sensuous and emotional apprehension and made sensuously apparent the darkest subtleties of his mind. This is the felt thought of Donne which one must grasp before any real understanding of his genius is possible; and Carew penetrates the secret which Johnson misses altogether.

Carew next refers to Donne's revolt against Elizabethan imitation and to his general service to poetry:

> The Muses garden with Pedantique weedes
> O'rspred, was purg'd by thee; the lazie seeds
> Of servile imitation throwne away;
> And fresh invention planted.

Continuing, he tells how poets were expected to be possessed with Pindar's fury, not their own, and to practice "The subtle cheat Of slie Exchanges" with the classics — perhaps a dig at Jonson, though probably at Elizabethan imitation in general. Donne's fresh invention was, to be possessed with his own fury and to draw upon experience and originality, or

> from those bare lands
> Of what is purely thine.

Carew heralds Donne as one who has enlarged the domain of poetry and has

> open'd Us a Mine
> Of rich and pregnant phansie, drawne a line
> Of masculine expression.

This mine was psychological experience as well as new sources of imagery discovered in it. The line of masculine expression came from Donne's effort to achieve significant expression in language. The struggle of his intellect with its medium is described by Carew, who recognizes that Donne's language lacks the "tun'd chime" which may charm the outward sense of posterity, but asserts

> Yet thou maist claime
> From so great disadvantage greater fame,
> Since to the awe of thy imperious wit
> Our stubborne language bends, made only fit
> With her tough-thick-rib'd hoopes to gird about
> Thy Giant phansie, which had prov'd too stout
> For their soft melting Phrases.

Here Carew defines not only the struggle of an imperious mind to achieve itself in language, but also the astringent effect which that mind had on the soft melting phrases of the followers of Spenser and Petrarch. Thus Donne created a music of ideas which charms the inward sense.

Apprehension lest the gods and goddesses whom Donne had exiled will be recalled is voiced by Carew, and lest classical tales again

> Shall stuffe their lines, and swell the windy Page,
> Till Verse refin'd by thee, in this last Age
> Turne ballad rime.

For their return, poetry had not long to wait. Indeed the simple measures which Donne and his school subtilized till the same metre could give the wonderfully various music of Marvell's *Coy Mistress* and

Crashaw's *Saint Teresa* did turn ballad rime in the less varied music of the classical couplet.

When we finish Carew's lament for the late king of the universal monarchy of wit, we realize that we have been reading incisive criticism. If Carew gives us the sympathetic contemporary view of the Donne tradition — and there is no reason to doubt it — he gives us a view that presents much less to quarrel with than that which Dr. Johnson gives. Calling attention to the sensuous thinking in Donne, his revolt against Elizabethan imitation, his introduction of new subject-matter and sources of imagery, his astringent intellect and its masculine music, his fire and giant fancy and subtle verse, Carew gives his poetry an abler and more modern analysis than either Dryden or Johnson achieved, and presents us with a lucid account of the Donne tradition as it began its career of influence.

The tradition which has appeared to us under the pen of Carew has often been denied, and even its possibility has been questioned by critics who have held that a lesser genius than Donne could not be successful in his style. But Carew, whose *Elegie* is so full of tribute to the fertilizing power of Donne's genius, recognized the difficulty of following him when he wrote:

> But thou art gone, and thy strict Lawes will be
> Too hard for Libertines in Poetrie.

And where success is difficult, but not impossible, the Metaphysical poets adventured; others have followed them; and so the tradition has been established. To justify it Marvell should be enough, but justification is not lacking in English poetry from Bishop King to T. S. Eliot. The nature of this tradition may be concisely defined as complex, sensuous, and intellectual as opposed to the simple, sensuous, and passionate tradition, if we remember that it does not exclude the rapture or passion of Sappho and Catullus. This may be not to define it at all.

What this influence meant for the seventeenth century, and came to mean for later times, in the practice of poets must be added to any estimate of the Donne tradition and its place in English poetry. Over its father, as if to challenge posterity, looms the admiring shadow of Ben Jonson, who gave the same high homage only to Shakspere and who never condescended to John Donne. It is with the other Johnson that criticism must chiefly rest its quarrel, though not without admiration.

III. CHAPMAN AND DONNE

A GLANCE at the background before which Donne appears as the witty monarch of the Metaphysical school is almost sure to raise the question, Was Donne the first Metaphysical poet? I am not concerned with the general European phenomenon in literary style of which Euphuism was the English manifestation, but I am concerned with any distinctly Metaphysical trait which may have appeared in Donne's immediate background. If we look for poets whose style is distinguished by obscurity — so commonly regarded as a Metaphysical quality — we are sure to come upon George Chapman and Fulke Greville. If we look for poets who represent the conflict between philosophy and poetry which exercised the Elizabethan mind and which Sidney expressed in his *Defence of Poesie*, we shall come upon still other poets who exhibit some quality of the Metaphysical. But we shall not find a poet like Donne, who represents the peculiar combination of qualities which impressed his contemporaries as something novel and later generations as the very type of the Metaphysical poet.

In Chapman, however, we must recognize a poet whose qualities have so much in common with the Metaphysical school that he might be called the first

Metaphysical poet. This kinship has already been noticed by one or two critics: by Professor F. L. Schoell in these words referring to Chapman's *Hymn to Christ upon the Cross*:

> Bref, Chapman se révèle dans ce poème ardu métaphysicien et grave dispensateur de "theological wit," et il est surprenant que nul critique, même pas Courthope, ne lui ait encore fait sa place aux côtés de Donne ou de John Davies of Hereford.[1]

But Schoell is mistaken in saying that this kinship has escaped critical notice, for T. S. Eliot had already placed Chapman by the side of Donne when Schoell wrote this.[2]

Chapman's earliest published verse is dated 1594, or one year later than the date commonly given for Donne's earliest verse, the *Satires*. Despite the difference in age, Chapman and Donne seem to have begun their poetic careers at almost the same time and with almost the same ideals; but Chapman had the advantage of publication. Like Jonson and Donne, he is a learned poet and stands somewhat apart from his time; among the three there is a certain intellectual community. But it is worth recalling that Marlowe exacted the homage of imitation from spirits so independent as Chapman[3] and Donne: from Chapman in the continuation of *Hero and Le-*

---

1. *Études sur l'humanisme continental en Angleterre*, p. 7.
2. The affinity between Chapman and Donne was first suggested, so far as I know, by Eliot in *The Sacred Wood*, p. 20.
3. Although Schoell has shown Chapman's extensive debt to Neo-Latin sources, Chapman was notably independent in his own age.

ander, and from Donne in *The Baite.* And we should
not forget that Marlowe also wrote the tragedy of
the learned man, of the man with "the hydroptic,
immoderate thirst of human learning" — Doctor
Faustus. It is not unlikely that the tragedy of erudition had its peculiar appeal for these two learned
poets.

Before looking at the qualities which Chapman
and Donne have in common, let us look at an extremely significant dedicatory epistle that Chapman
wrote for *Ovid's Banquet of Sense,* which he published
in 1595. In our day it would be considered hardly
less than a literary manifesto after the manner, let us
say, of the Imagist poets. Coming when it did, one
wonders whether it escaped being something like that
for the Metaphysical poets, since it states so many of
the things for which those poets were afterwards distinguished.[1] One can hardly believe that young John
Donne did not read it and approve. Let me give
some of its most significant dicta:[2]

The profane multitude I hate, and only consecrate my
strange poems to those searching spirits, whom learning
hath made noble, and nobility sacred.

Such is the audience to which this poetry is addressed. What appears to be a typical humanistic
boast will later recall the pride which Donne's audi-

1. Herbert Read suggests the importance of this epistle in a footnote
to his essay on "The Nature of Metaphysical Poetry," *The Criterion,*
vol. i, no. 3, p. 255.
2. *Works of George Chapman* (ed. Shepherd, 1874), *Minor Poems,*
pp. 21–22.

ence has taken in understanding him. The nature of these strange poems is elaborated in this passage:

That *Energia*, or clearness of representation, required in absolute poems, is not the perspicuous delivery of a low invention; but high and hearty invention expressed in most significant and unaffected phrase . . . and in my opinion, that which being with a little endeavour searched, adds a kind of majesty to Poesy, is better than that which every cobbler may sing to his patch.

The use of obscurity and conceits is then set forth:

Obscurity in affection of words and indigested conceits, is pedantical and childish; but where it shroudeth itself in the heart of his subject, uttered with fitness of figure and expressive epithets, with that darkness will I still labour to be shadowed.

Referring directly to his patron, Matthew Roydon, Chapman adds,

You have actual means to sound the philosophical conceits, that my new pen so seriously courteth.

And, in anticipation of criticism, Chapman concludes:

I know that empty and dark spirits will complain of palpable night; but those that beforehand have a radiant and light-bearing intellect, will say they can pass through Corinna's garden without the help of a lantern.

In these dicta we have a very direct statement of qualities that came to be synonymous with Metaphysical poetry.

Seldom has the intellectual strain in poetry had a more forthright vindication, more amazing even because it came hard upon the simple, sensuous music of Spenser's *Epithalamion*. Such a revolt against the easy verse "which every cobbler may sing to his patch" cannot have escaped the eye of Donne, himself an enemy of Elizabethan facility. Intellectual energy, the philosophical conceit, and the darkness that is the shadow of thought, all of which characterize Donne's poetry, are here set forth by Chapman as his poetic ideals; and however he may bungle in his "tenebrous" style, they are the ideals which govern his practice, beginning with *Ovid's Banquet of Sense*. Yet another side of the intellectual nature of his poetry is presented by the poems with which this manifesto is connected. Their inspiration and metaphors are largely derived from his reading; earlier, he even went so far as to append to *The Shadow of Night* a gloss of all the learning embodied in its poetry. Like Donne, Chapman got a thrill from his reading that other poets get from life; as T. S. Eliot remarks, "their mode of feeling was directly and freshly altered by their reading and thought." [1] For this reason Chapman consecrated his "strange poems to those searching spirits, whom learning hath made noble."

The intellectual community between Chapman and Donne is suggested by the motto which Chapman attached to this booklet of 1595: "Quis leget haec? Nemo Hercule Nemo, vel duo vel nemo: Persius." [2] It is generally held that Persius furnished the model

1. *Homage to John Dryden*, p. 29.
2. *Works of George Chapman* (ed. Shepherd, 1874), *Minor Poems*, p. 20.

of style for Donne's *Satires*.[1] Of course this common reference to Persius does nothing more than suggest, like the imitation of Marlowe, a certain affinity between two minds, which appeared more concretely in Chapman's statement of Metaphysical poetry. Yet it is more than likely that the style of Persius, which Coleridge defined as "hard — not obscure," had a definite influence on the shaping of Chapman's poetic principles, which both he and Donne exemplified, not less because Donne probably went directly to Persius for the style of his *Satires*.[2] Furthermore, we know that a fate similar to that which Chapman anticipates in his dedicatory epistle actually overtook Donne's verse when his admirers, whose radiant and light-bearing intellect enabled them to pass through Corinna's garden without the help of a lantern, boasted that his verse was

> Indeed so farre above its Reader, good,
> That wee are thought wits, when 't is understood.[3]

But the contents of *Ovid's Banquet of Sense* and its companion poems have other evidence of the kinship of mind, and even hints of influence, between Chapman and Donne.

1. Yet Dryden says that "he followed Horace so very close, that of necessity he must fall with him." Ed. Ker, i, 102.

2. Peacham's *Compleat Gentleman* of 1622 supports this idea: "Persius, I know not why we should so much affect him, since with his obscuritie hee laboureth not to affect us; yet in our learned age he is now discovered to every Schoole-boie: his stile is broken, froward, unpleasing, and harsh." Spingarn, *Critical Essays of the Seventeenth Century*, i, 127.

This is a valuable side-light on the critical mind of the age which held Donne in such high esteem.

3. *On Dr. Donnes death*, Grierson, *Donne's Poetical Works*, i, 382.

This publication contains the following items: *"Ouid's Banquet of Sence. A Coronet for his Mistresse Philosophie, and his amorous Zodiacke.* With a translation of a Latine coppie, written by a Fryer, Anno Dom. 1400."* In what Swinburne calls the "sensual metaphysics"[1] of *Ovid's Banquet of Sense* one cannot but see a parallel to Donne, especially to his early love poetry; in the same way learning is mingled with the life of the senses. Professor Schoell describes this poem in these words:

> Toute occasion lui est bonne pour faire parade d'une érudition qui ne va pas "sans pointes" et formuler des sentences qui ne sont pas exemptes de "concetti." Et surtout le poème fourmille de comparaisons savantes empruntées à la physique, à la philosophie ou à la mythologie.[2]

This is the effect of a kiss:

> And as a pebble cast into a spring,
> We see a sort of trembling circles rise
> One forming other in their issuing,
> Till over all the fount they circulize;
>   So this perpetual-motion-making kiss
> Is propagate through all my faculties.[3]

And if one would see thought disarming modesty in the very manner of *The Extasie,* here is a fine example:

> As in your sight, how can sight simply being
> A sense receiving essence to his flame,
> Sent from his object, give it harm by seeing
> Whose action in the seer hath his frame?[4]

---

1. Swinburne, Introduction to *Works of Chapman* (1874), *Minor Poems,* p. xxl.   2. *Op. cit.,* p. 38.
3. *Works of Chapman* (1874), *Minor Poems,* p. 35, col. 1.
4. *Ibid.,* p. 32, col. 2.

Nothing could be closer than this "philosophical conceit" to the very shape of the Donne conceit and to the very manner of Donne's thinking.

Chapman's figures, like Donne's, are often drawn from his reading, as in this passage:

> O that as intellects themselves transite,
> To each intelligible quality,
>   My life might pass into my love's conceit
> Thus to be form'd in words, her tunes, and breath,
> And with her kisses sing itself to death.[1]

In these examples one can see the relation of sense to mind, of body to soul, which *Ovid's Banquet of Sense* develops and which is to be found at the centre of Donne's thought. For both poets this conclusion will serve:

> Minds taint no more with bodies' touch or tire,
> Than bodies nourish with the mind's desire.[2]

Reading this poem and remembering that it was published in 1595, we may be permitted to wonder at its likeness to the poetry of Donne.

Before we leave it, let me illustrate a use of the conceit that challenges the worst in Crashaw:

> Love's feet are in his eyes; for if he please
> The depth of beauty's gulfy flood to sound,
>   He goes upon his eyes.[3]

As a contrast, here is the conceit used in the best Donne fashion:

> Contentment is our heaven, and all our deeds
> Bend in that circle, seld' or never closed.[4]

1. *Ibid.*, p. 25, col. 2.   2. *Ibid.*, p. 35, col. 2.
3. *Ibid.*, p. 24, col. 1.   4. *Ibid.*, p. 29, col. 2.

We may think, not unreasonably, that *Ovid's Banquet of Sense* is in itself enough to establish the intellectual community between Chapman and Donne.[1]

But *A Coronet for his Mistress Philosophy* presents more interesting evidence for this conclusion. For its subject is that whereby any poet is metaphysical, from the truly universal sort like Dante to the more restricted sort like Donne, because each finds his inspiration in learning.[2] Here is that Philosophy which captured Dante, and more and more of Donne as he grew older — she whom Chapman describes in these lines:

> Her mind — the beam of God — draws in the fires
> Of her chaste eyes, from all earth's tempting fuel.[3]

As fine a conceit as this is of the Donne sort, it is an even finer description of the change, always implicit, in Donne's thought which time brought about. It looks forward to the time when Donne, identifying woman and philosophy and confronted with the task of commemorating Elizabeth Drury, could approach his work in the spirit of these lines:

> Yet shall my active and industrious pen
> Wind his sharp forehead through those parts that raise her,
> And register her worth past rarest women.[4]

This was the alternative that Chapman proposed to singing "Love's sensual empery," which he had sung

---

1. See Appendix C for other examples of the conceit in this poem.
2. Schoell, speaking of Chapman's poetry, says, "Or, cette dernière plonge d'aussi profondes racines dans la métaphysique du moyen âge que celle de Donne, par exemple." *Op. cit.*, p. 19.
3. *Op. cit.*, p. 38, col. 2.   4. *Ibid.*, p. 39, col. 2.

in *Ovid's Banquet of Sense*. If Donne saw this *Coronet*, he must have been tremendously impressed, especially since it is conveyed in his favorite manner of writing. Chapman returns to his dictum on Metaphysical poetry in these lines on philosophy:

> And like the pansy, with a little veil,
> She gives her inward work the greater grace;
> Which my lines imitate, though much they fail
> Her gifts so high, and times' conceit so base.[1]

And when Philosophy, speaking through Chapman, says,

> But my love is the cordial of souls,
> Teaching by passion what perfection is,[2]

we can almost hear Donne himself speaking from his subtle heart.

I cannot leave *A Coronet for his Mistress Philosophy* without mentioning a peculiarity of its form: it is a corona or circlet of sonnets. Of course this reminds us of Donne's *La Corona* sonnets, which I agree with Grierson in placing at least as early as 1607. It is necessary to remember that Daniel published sonnets with a similar linking in 1594, which may be the source of Chapman's use of the circlet, as well as of Donne's later use. But because of the nature of Chapman's verse, I am inclined to believe that Donne took the idea for *La Corona* from him, though Chapman uses Daniel's rhyme scheme and Donne does not, except for a few lines.

1. *Ibid.*   2. *Ibid.*, p. 38, col. 1.

Donne was notoriously independent, as we know, and hence arises the difficulty of his kinship with Chapman, who was the older man. If they knew one another, it was probably through Jonson. If they did not, it is far more probable that Donne read Chapman's published verse than that Chapman read Donne's manuscript poems, since Donne at this time certainly was not so definitely launched as a poet. At the publication of this Metaphysical volume, with its highly significant dedicatory epistle, Chapman was probably already a playwright; at any rate, so typical a play as the later *Bussy D'Ambois* shows the sort of image that we find in *Ovid's Banquet of Sense*.[1] But the direction of this influence, or whether it was an influence at all, is much less important than what it does for Donne. It removes from him the character of an eccentric in English poetry and relates him to certain elements in the dramatic and lyric verse of the late Elizabethan and early Jacobean poets.

Thus Chapman becomes a link which permits us to see how the current of poetry descended in a direct line to the Metaphysical poets. He was the oldest of the late Elizabethans, and was alive to the poetic tendencies of his time. Both his lyric and his dramatic verse[2] represent the elements that I have pointed out as later belonging to Metaphysical poetry and that are found in the development — or, as

---

1. See Appendix C for examples of the conceit in *Bussy D'Ambois*; *The Revenge* will afford like examples.
2. See Appendix C for their common image.

it is sometimes called, the degeneration — of sensibility in the late Elizabethan dramatic verse. In this verse Mr. Wells has shown the abundant presence of the Radical image or conceit, and, from his study, has reached this conclusion: "In Donne and his followers and in the plays of Webster, Marston, Chapman, Tourneur and Shakespere, Radical metaphor reached its crest. In the more conservative Spenser it is scarcely to be found." [1] With Shakspere the omnipresent, this group illustrates the correlation I have suggested; the conclusion about Spenser is important because of his probable significance for Chapman and Donne.

The common elements of this lyric and dramatic poetry are also illustrated in the conceits which Webster borrows for his *Duchess of Malfi* from the lyric verse of Chapman and Donne. Mr. Charles Crawford presents an interesting garner of these images in his *Collectanea*.[2] The peculiar ability of the conceit to conjure poetry out of the prosaic, even the ugly, appears in these borrowings to express the so-called decadent sensibility of late Elizabethan drama, as in this instance:

th' embroidery
Wrought on his state, is like a leprosy,
The whiter, still the fouler.
(Chapman, "A Great Man," p. 149, col. 1)

1. *Poetic Imagery*, p. 136. This conclusion is supported by Eliot's statement in *Homage to John Dryden*, p. 26, ll. 2–6.
2. *Second Series:* "Montaigne, Webster, and Marston: Donne and Webster," pp. 54–63. Shows very illuminating connections.

> Methinks her fault and beauty,
> Blended together, show like leprosy,
> The whiter, the fouler.
>
> (*Duchess of Malfi*, III, iii, 76–78)

When emotions thus got subtler and more complex, introspective and intellectualized, they sought expression in the subtle conceit; and when dramatists like Webster and Marston incorporated their reading — for instance, Montaigne — into their verse, they did exactly what Donne and Chapman did in their Metaphysical poetry; and, again like them, they resorted to the conceit in this incorporation.[1]

By seeing the connection between Chapman and Donne, whichever way the influence went, we see Donne no longer as an isolated phenomenon, but as a poet in the current of English poetry. For Chapman connects him with late Elizabethan dramatic verse, and Webster's borrowings reveal the elements common to that verse and to Donne. An instructive comparison could be made between the verse offered by these dramatists and that offered by the Metaphysicals as a monument to Prince Henry. It is significant that the "curiously thoughtful and ingenious" [2] character of Chapman's images caught the eye of Swinburne just as the Metaphysical images drew the rhetoric of Dr. Johnson. And when Swinburne also remarks the opulence of figure in Chapman,[3] we are

1. Crawford, *op. cit.* Here may be found valuable supporting material for this conclusion, showing the operation of their sensibility.
2. Swinburne, *op. cit.*, p. xix.
3. *Ibid.*

reminded of the same wealth in the Metaphysical poets. Another quality of Chapman's verse that Swinburne notices has its parallel both in the dramatic verse of the time and in Donne: that is the "convulsive movement of the broken and jarring sentences." [1] The growing irregularity in the dramatic verse of late Elizabethan and early Jacobean times has often been noticed, and the roughness of Donne is notorious, but the relation between the two has seldom drawn sufficient attention.

Mr. T. S. Eliot has observed that verse at the beginning of the seventeenth century exhibits "the constant suggestion and the skilful evasion of iambic pentameter." [2] Professor Saintsbury has called our attention to the symptoms of degeneration both latent and active in blank verse during the first part of the seventeenth century; at the same time he has held that the lyric preserved its original integrity.[3] Some of the means which brought about degeneration as they ceased to be avenues to supreme achievement were the run-on line, the varied pause, the trisyllabic foot, and the redundant syllable. These are the means that carried Shakspere from the single-moulded line to the verse-clause and verse-paragraph which are part of his achievement.

Now Donne is no exception to the use of such means in the couplet; nor does he escape them in the lyric. And certainly there is much in Praz's claim

1. *Ibid.*, p. xiii.
2. "Reflections on Vers Libre," *New Statesman*, 3 March, 1917.
3. *History of English Prosody*, vol. ii, especially inter-chap. 5 and chap. 4 of book vi.

that Donne built his verse on the rhythmical basis of the stanza or paragraph rather than of the single verse, for this agrees with the assertion of the rights of intellect which is apparent in his verse. This assertion of content is paralleled, I believe, in the evolution of Shakspere's blank verse from the single-moulded line to the verse-paragraph. Moreover, the degradation of blank verse was probably not unconnected with the tendency toward realism that comes out in the approximation of Donne's poetry to colloquial directness and in the ability of the conceit to make use of prosaic material. Something of this correlation may be felt in a notion that Webster borrows from Donne:

> *Card.* I do not think but sorrow makes her look
> Like to an oft-dy'd garment.
> > (*Duchess of Malfi*, V, ii, 120–121)

> > summers robe growes
> Duskie, and like an oft dyed garment showes.
> > (*First Anniversary*, ll. 355–356)[1]

The same transforming forces are at work in these lines of dramatic and of lyric verse; they indicate a relationship that we must reckon with.

And Chapman is the link that connects Donne most intimately with these transforming forces. Of these forces the *energia* of Chapman's dedicatory epistle is the strongest, and is recognized in the criticism which Professor Boas gives of his style:

---

1. Cited by Crawford, *op. cit.*, pp. 60–61.

Thus Chapman aimed throughout at energy of expression at all costs. To this he sacrificed beauty of phrase and rhythm, even lucidity . . . in fact many of the difficulties spring from excessive condensation.[1]

This is the result of that *energia*, of that "high and hearty invention expressed in most significant and unaffected phrase." Notice the stress of invention, which leads to ingenuity; of significant expression, which makes meaning paramount; and of unaffected phrase, which encourages the sacrifice of beauty of phrase and the subordination of rhythm to energy. Most apt in the expression of such qualities, as I have tried to show, is the Radical image which produces such energy and leads to such condensation. It gives vitality to the dramatic verse of these late Elizabethan and early Jacobean poets, and it connects them with Donne. Furthermore, it reveals in these poets the operation that Dr. Johnson remarked in a late Metaphysical poet: "Botany in the mind of Cowley turned into poetry." Such was also their relation to learning. Of these things, Chapman and Donne were not isolated expressions, but rather the most individualized and conscious.

If we choose to call these qualities disintegrating forces, like the new knowledge of the time, we may also see in them the assertion of the philosophic side of the conflict between philosophy and poetry which troubled the Elizabethan mind. To these forces or to this assertion, Donne brought the most powerful

1. Introduction to *Bussy D'Ambois and The Revenge* (Belles Lettres Series, 1905), pp. xxvi–xxvii.

and individual mind. Without him English poetry would be much the poorer in original achievement and in fertilizing genius. But great as the novelty of his talent is, it is related to a development of sensibility that operated profoundly in late Elizabethan times.

IV. PROLOGUE TO THE
SUCCESSION

THE LINE of the Metaphysicals in the seventeenth century becomes distinct in the influence of poet upon poet, deriving more or less directly from Donne, but remaining a thing of individuals rather than of a school, till it attains something like critical consciousness in the mind of Dryden.[1] Nowhere else in the criticism of the century shall we find a hint of a school of poets headed by Donne, much less of the Metaphysical school. But in Carew and others we do find a perception of the magnificent isolation of Donne with respect to the prevailing mould of Elizabethan poetry; and in seventeenth-century poetry, admitting its common roots in medievalism, classicism, scholasticism, Petrarchism, concettism, and Euphuism, we find him to be of even more compelling genius than he appeared to his contemporaries. Though we shall find the most vivid testimony to his reputation in the verse which followed him, we cannot neglect the figure he cut in seventeenth-century criticism, nor can we overlook the story which printing tells of the seasons of his popularity.[2]

Donne's critical reputation begins with Ben Jonson's conversations with Drummond of Hawthornden

1. See Appendix A for a chronology of inheritance.
2. See Appendix B for seventeenth-century editions of Donne's verse.

in 1618, when Jonson declared that Donne was "the first poet in the world in some things"; that "Done, for not keeping of accent, deserved hanging"; and that "Done . . . for not being understood, would perish." In 1633 Carew's *Elegie*, as we have already seen, described Donne as an innovator in both subject-matter and style, and implied the roughness which Jonson named. The numerous *Elegies upon the Author* in Grierson's edition of Donne repeat Carew in part and chant a hymn of praise to the king of wit; this is also true of Lord Herbert's elegy on Donne, which Grierson for some reason omits. These elegies are not wanting in subtlety of observation, as Sidney Godolphin shows when he calls Donne, "Pious dissector." But the eighteenth century would certainly have read in a literal fashion this couplet from Mr. Mayne:

> And when we most come neere thee, 't is our blisse
> To imitate thee, where thou dost amisse.[1]

And in 1640 Walton's *Life*, while emphasizing Donne's religious career as the centre of his reputation, calls attention to his "sharp wit and high fancy" and "his choice metaphors."

From the Restoration to the end of the century, biographers, with the exception of Dryden, combine previous criticism, adding hardly more than a phrase or so, and continuing the tradition of Donne as a poet of great wit and learning, though of some harshness, but losing sight of his intensity of poetic

---

1. *On Dr. Donnes death*, Grierson, *Donne's Poetical Works*, i, 383.

feeling.[1] Biographers like Edward Phillips[2] and William Winstanley[3] did not come near the critical perception of the early elegists, who, it seems to me, saw most of the things we see in Donne. Further evidence of such perception may be found in lines like this from Izaak Walton,

> Did his youth scatter *Poetrie*, wherein
> Was all Philosophie?[4]

and in discriminations like this from Arthur Wilson,

> Thy nimble *Satyres* too, and every strainc
> (With nervy strength) that issued from thy brain.[5]

The reprinting of Donne tells us a story similar to that of the critical wavering of his reputation, which went into a definite decline with the Restoration. Between 1633 and 1655 six editions of his complete poetical works were printed; after these but one complete edition appeared, that of 1669, until Tonson's edition in 1719. This list does not include an edition of the *Satires* in 1662 or Huyghen's Dutch translation, the *Koren-bloemen* of 1672. Judging from the editions, one must conclude that Donne's reputation has never come so near eclipse as between the Restoration and the end of the century. Even the truly antagonistic eighteenth century has at least Pope's

---

1. See Arthur H. Nethercot's very useful article on "The Reputation of the 'Metaphysical Poets' during the Seventeenth Century," *Jour. Engl. and Ger. Phil.*, vol. xxiii (1924); especially pp. 175–177.
2. *Theatrum Poetarum Anglicanorum* (1675).
3. *The Lives of the Most Famous English Poets* (1687).
4. Grierson, *op. cit.*, i, 376.
5. *Ibid.*, p. 385.

modernizations and three editions of Donne's poems
to show for this period's one.[1] This is all the more
surprising because the rather frequent reprinting of
Walton's *Life* must have served to keep Donne's
memory alive. This decline in his reputation will be
explained when we consider him in relation to the
new influence which centres in Dryden. For the
present we need merely to recognize that, neglecting the *Anniversaries* and the numerous manuscript
copies, the editions of Donne's poems cover a span
from 1633 to 1669, which is the range of the Metaphysical poets and the period of his dominant influence. But we must not forget that to the general
reader the only apparent bond between the Metaphysical poets was their devotional verse, though
we must except from this generalization the poets
whose elegies show that they were conscious of the
manner and style of Donne.

The Donne who was a friend to several of the
Caroline poets and a legend to the others has been
clearly drawn for us in Carew's *Elegie*, which praises
wit as his special glory. All those poets who addressed
verses to Donne — such as Herbert, Lord Herbert,
Bishop King, even Jonson — are inclined to this
opinion. It remained for another tradition to label
this wit "metaphysical" and to look at it with the
complacence which every age has for its immediate
predecessor. Seeking to avoid such complacence and
prejudicial scorn, I have tried to show how intimately
related this wit is to poetic surprise and the conceit,

1. See Geoffrey Keynes, *Bibliography of John Donne*, pp. 105–125.

how intellectual it is in fibre, and how it serves to make the familiar strange, and the strange familiar, which Coleridge attributed to the office of good poetry. The object of this wit has never been better defined than it was by Sir Henry Craik, "not to excite laughter but to compel attention"; [1] and this object was achieved largely through the conceit, which represents a particular way of thinking and feeling. I have also tried to show how Donne brought the method of psychological realism to his new subject-matter and a rational evolution to the structure of his poems. At the same time I have indicated the effect of intellect upon his verse, the nature of his revolt against Petrarchianism, the form of his poetic mind, and the general character of his tradition as it appeared to the Caroline poets.

How these poets sprang to the banner of Donne is a matter of history. The difficulty that one encounters in tracing the line of the Metaphysicals comes when one attempts to say what poets practice Metaphysical poetry and in what manner. My purpose shall be not to exhaust the catalogue of Metaphysical poets, but to suggest the character of this influence in figures who give continuity to the tradition down to the death of Cowley. For the sake of clearness, I shall mark out the tradition according to the two main subjects of Donne — love and religion. In the sacred line I shall discuss Herbert, Crashaw, and Vaughan; in the profane line I shall consider Lord Herbert, Bishop King, Marvell, and Townshend. The

1. Cited by Saintsbury, *Caroline Poets*, iii, 219.

flaws in this second grouping are patent, but not serious enough to destroy the opposition to the more homogeneous side of the tradition. In the seventeenth century these two lines of poetic filiation will be found, with certain fusions and conflicts with other traditions, to be of prime importance in any discussion of the Donne influence. Apart from these poets, the chief offenders in this style, Cleveland, Benlowes, and Cowley, will engage our attention; and then the fringe of the tradition and the reaction in Dryden.

Before, however, we can plunge into this discussion, we need to examine with greater particularity the image and the feeling which characterize the Metaphysical sensibility.

The Conceit

The conceit has so often been taken as the stigma of the Metaphysical poet that we owe it some scrutiny in this light. The difficulty which we have in defining it, and in recognizing it in many instances, should make us wary of asserting it to be essentially different from the normal poetic figure. Although Bacon and Jonson used the term *conceit* for the thought itself, it soon came to be identified with a far-fetched image, and later to be associated exclusively with Donne and his school. In view of this historical fate, and since we have seen how necessary the conceit is to Donne's peculiar mode of thinking and feeling, we cannot afford to neglect it as a criterion of the Donne tradition.

To this end let me give a few attempts to define the conceit. Mr. R. M. Alden gives this definition: "A conceit is the elaboration of a verbal or an imaginative figure, or the substitution of a logical for an imaginative figure, with so considerable a use of an intellectual process as to take precedence, at least for the moment, of the normal poetic process." [1] He recognizes this danger: "One must admit that the intervention of an intellectual process (the essence of our definition), in threatening to suspend our imaginative sympathy with the poet's main course of feeling, imperils his success." [2] This definition covers the fibre of thought which we feel to be most characteristic of Donne's figure, but it does not cover Crashaw's use of "opening the purple wardrobe in thy side," or Lovelace's use of "green ice," or Vaughan's use of "virgin-crummes" as applied to the Innocents, for these figures have that touch of the fantastic which derives from the imaginative distance between the things associated. Nor will it cover similar figures in Donne. Here the suspension of our imaginative sympathy comes less from intellectual intervention than from imaginative distance that is greater than poetry ordinarily requires us to leap.

A test for the conceit that infers a definition like the one just given has been formulated by Mr. G. H. Palmer: "Does it by thought exclude feeling, or

1. "The Lyrical Conceits of the Elizabethans," *Studies in Philology*, vol. xiv, no. 2, p. 137.
2. *Ibid.*, pp. 151–152.

does it through thought embody feeling in some new, individual, and subtle way?" [1] This also places the accent on thought, but it has the merit of admitting the conceit as a means of representing a particular way of thinking and feeling. Both of these definitions recognize a certain intellectual difficulty in the conceit that endangers the feeling, and both fail to account for a surprise that is primarily imaginative.

After making a study of conceits, Miss Kathleen M. Lea comes to this conclusion: "The 'metaphysical' poets regarded the simile as a useful, not as an ornamental, device: and the conceits of their poetry were due to under-emphasis." [2] Under-emphasis as compared with the Elizabethan over-emphasis of the simile. Miss Lea finds that even when Donne stumbles upon loveliness his image is still subsidiary to the thought. Surely this is not a weakness! For the reverse is the charge most commonly made against the conceit. But in this definition also the conceit serves as the embodiment of feeling, not as its ornament; hence the emphasis falls upon expression.

The typical image of Donne has been called the Radical image by Mr. Henry W. Wells, who defines it thus: "Radical imagery occurs where two terms of a metaphor meet on a limited ground, and are otherwise definitely incongruent. It makes daring excursions into the seemingly commonplace. The

1. *The English Works of George Herbert* (1905), i, 161.
2. "Conceits," *Modern Language Review*, vol. xx, no. 4 (October, 1925), p. 398.

minor term promises little imaginative value. In a coldness to apparently incongruent suggestion this figure approaches the neutral comparison, while in ingenuity it approaches the conceit."[1] This definition is illustrated by the figure of the compasses. Mr. Wells further illustrates the Radical image as a figure of close analysis, as an essential medium of expression for Donne's exploration of the soul, and as a natural resort of the realist and mystic. To me this definition is especially cogent because, in laying stress on the lack of intrinsic imaginative value in the minor term of the Radical image, it accounts for the imaginative distance between the terms of a conceit and thus gives us a means of distinguishing what seems to be a conceit lacking the fundamental brain work that we have noticed.

In these definitions we may observe a certain agreement that the conceit is characterized by fundamental brain work and subordinance to expression, and in the last one we have a recognition of the imaginative distance which seems to me so important a trait of the conceit. In comparison with the normal poetic figure, the conceit does retard, if not actually suspend, our imaginative sympathy with the poet's main course of feeling. But this retarding of our imaginative comprehension may derive from two sources: the intellectual difficulty of the figure, or the unusual imaginative distance between the things connected. The justification of this retarded sympathy must come from the nature of the

1. *Poetic Imagery*, p. 31.

feeling itself. This brings us to the question of sincerity in language.

Of poetic language Mr. T. E. Hulme has this to say: "If it is sincere in the accurate sense, when the whole of the analogy is necessary to get out the exact curve of the feeling or thing you want to express — there you seem to me to have the highest verse, even though the subject be trivial and the emotions of the infinite far away." [1] This is the test of sincerity which the conceit, as well as the normal poetic figure, must meet. And in Donne the conceit will generally meet this test, for the conceit is there a structural decoration: it supports the feeling.

Thus we may say that the conceit retards our imaginative comprehension because it is necessary to get out the exact curve of Donne's mode of thinking and feeling; and that mode embraced intense passion, intellectual difficulty, and unusual imaginative connections. Somewhat as the resistance of the wire may bring out the heat in an electric current, the conceit in Donne brings out the exact curve of his feeling. By running his feeling through a term of little intrinsic imaginative value he succeeds in bringing out the full heat of his passion or the exact turn of his thought. Now let us apply these distinctions to some of his conceits.

> Thus vent thy thoughts; abroad I'll studie thee,
>   As he removes farre off, that great heights takes;
>   How great love is, presence best tryall makes,
> But absence tryes how long this love will bee;

1. *Speculations*, p. 138.

> To take a latitude
> Sun, or starres, are fitliest view'd
> At their brightest, but to conclude
> Of longitudes, what other way have wee,
> But to marke when, and where the darke eclipses bee?[1]

Here the heat of Donne's emotion is made to glow through a complex figure involving neutral terms and exactly tracing his subtle thought; and as our imaginative comprehension is retarded, the feeling burns itself in. Besides, the image itself gives us a kind of intellectual pleasure.

In a less subtle image we may see more clearly the imaginative distance which seems to me so necessary to a definition of the conceit:

> Therefore I'll give no more; But I'll undoe
> The world by dying; because love dies too.
> Then all your beauties will bee no more worth
> Then gold in Mines, where none doth draw it forth;
> And all your graces no more use shall have
>   Then a Sun dyall in a grave.[2]

The sudden swoop at the end to the figure of a sundial in a grave gives us the same kind of shock that we experience in coming upon "a bracelet of bright haire about the bone," for the imaginative distance in each case is unusual and disturbing to the normal poetic process. The intellectual factor is not the dominant one in conceits of this type.

But if we turn to the conclusion of that wonderful first *Holy Sonnet*, we shall find both the imaginative

1. *A Valediction: of the booke*, Grierson, *op. cit.*, i, 31.
2. *The Will*, Grierson, *op. cit.*, i, 57.

distance and the fundamental brain work inextricably
mingled with the emotional intensity of Donne:

> But our old subtle foe so tempteth me,
> That not one houre my selfe I can sustaine;
> Thy Grace may wing me to prevent his art,
> And thou like Adamant draw mine iron heart.

This last line, one of the finest lines in Donne, is a
complete vindication of the conceit as a means of expressing a particular way of thinking and feeling.
Furthermore, it is a justification of poetry if we recall
T. E. Hulme's words on poetry: "It is a compromise
for a language of intuition which would hand over
sensations bodily. It always endeavors to arrest you,
and to make you continuously see a physical thing, to
prevent you gliding through an abstract process." [1]
If the conceit retards your gliding through an abstract process more than the normal image, it is because the exact curve of the feeling requires the
slower and more difficult path. When this test of
sincerity is not met, the conceit becomes as hollow
as any empty image and more reprehensible because
more assuming, for its object is not only to achieve
fineness of expression but to compel attention.

This very compelling of attention becomes the
chief source of weakness in the conceit when it fails
to meet the test of sincerity, since it calls attention
to its own defect. Another source of weakness comes
from another source of strength. As we have noticed,
part of the force of the conceit comes from its ability

1. *Op. cit.*, p. 134.

to conjure a powerful metaphorical relation out of a minor term of little poetic connotation, and conversely to neutralize a minor term whose connotation would impair or destroy the effect of the conceit. It is the failure to neutralize such terms that defeats the serious intent of many of the conceits of Donne's followers, though few of Donne's own. This is the case in Vaughan's use of "virgin-crummes" as applied to the Innocents, but not in Donne's use of "God's commissary" as applied to Fate. The Metaphysical poets are so concerned with the expression of their secondary sense that they frequently neglect the suggestions of their primary sense or even the emotional congruity. But when the conceit fails emotionally, it seldom fails to give us a kind of intellectual pleasure. In fact, the conceit, like the figure in science, scores through analysis and precision; it is a figure of close intellectual texture, for which Dr. Johnson rebuked it; but it may convey powerful emotion while neglecting intrinsic beauty.

Looking at the conceit in Donne, we were able to distinguish two varieties: the expanded conceit, which appears in the famous figure of the compasses; and the condensed conceit, which appears in "a Sun dyall in a grave" and makes striking use of the imaginative distance I have tried to define. The condensed conceit also plays a part in a kind of development characteristic of Donne's verse: that is a development by the rapid association of thought and image which requires agility of mind for its comprehension. It may be seen in Cowley's poem

Against Hope and in such a stanza as this from Donne's *Valediction: of weeping*:

> On a round ball
> A workeman that hath copies by, can lay
> An Europe, Afrique, and an Asia,
> And quickly make that, which was nothing, *All*,
> So doth each teare,
> Which thee doth weare,
> A globe, yea world by that impression grow,
> Till thy teares mixt with mine doe overflow
> This world, by waters sent from thee, my heaven
> dissolved so.

To quote Dr. Johnson, "The tears of lovers are always of great poetical account; but Donne has extended them into worlds." Here the thought is developed by the rapid association of the images of the geographer's globe, the tear, and the deluge. Admitting the demand for agility on the part of the reader, it seems to me idle to deny that these images and this development represent a particular way of thinking and feeling, and are completely referable to the exact curve of that feeling. In fact, it is through such means that these poets achieve what one may call the Metaphysical shudder, and this seems to me a quality of emotion that is peculiar to their mode of thought.

We may conclude that the conceit does not exist for itself, as has been too often said, but for the thought and feeling which it is to embody. Our consciousness of the intellectual process involved in the conceit is a witness to its primary function as expression. Since its object is not only to achieve fineness of expression but also to compel attention, we need not be surprised that one of its aims requires agility of mind on the part of the reader and the other reveals itself in intellectual or imaginative surprise. There is fundamental brain work in the true Donne conceit, which retards our imaginative sympathy with the poet's main course of feeling, but does not suspend it unless his figure fails. His conceit is not a decoration, but a structural decoration which supports his feeling and interprets his thought.

Like Donne, the Metaphysical poets do not keep their images on one side and their meanings on another, but subordinate their images to their meanings; in other words, they make their images say what they mean. This is by no means true of all poets. As T. S. Eliot has remarked, "when Shelley has some definite statement to make, he simply says it; keeps his images on one side and his meanings on the other." [1] Now the definite statements of the Metaphysical poets are never simply said. To test this conclusion, compare *The Weeper* of Crashaw with *The Skylark* of Shelley, or compare *The Retreat* of Vaughan with the *Immortality Ode* of Wordsworth, or read Wordsworth's *Ode to Duty*, where the division between images and meanings is even more definite. In the difference here suggested, we discover the sensuous thinking that I have tried to show in Donne, the thinking in which the image is the

1. "The Poems of Richard Crashaw," *The Dial*, vol. lxxxiv, no. 3 (March, 1928), p. 249.

body of the thought rather than a thing of beauty in itself. In this sensuous thinking the images are not merely illustrative, they advance the intellectual progress of the poem.

The distinctions which I have made probably justify us in calling Donne's image the conceit, but they do not exempt the conceit from the legitimate tests of poetic imagery. Nor do they distinguish it in essential nature from the normal image. This much may be said: the conceit ordinarily shows more brain work, makes larger use of material of little innate poetic value, and achieves greater imaginative distance. Which is to explain why it is commonly regarded as difficult, perverse, and far-fetched. If we will regard it as indispensable to a particular mode of thinking and feeling, we shall understand the Metaphysical poets as they were understood, which is no more than all poets require. It is in this light that we must regard the conceit as a criterion of the Donne tradition.

The Metaphysical Shudder

There is a quality of emotion that seems to me peculiar to the Metaphysical mode of thought. This I have called the Metaphysical shudder. It is difficult to analyze, but, once felt, it can never be forgotten; and it is most precisely concentrated in Donne.

In biography it is represented by Donne and his shroud. However, as T. S. Eliot so aptly remarks, "Donne and his shroud, the shroud and his motive

for wearing it, are inseparable, but they are not the
same thing." [1] The shroud belonged to his time.
What a place it held in that age we can see in the
Urn-Burial of Sir Thomas Browne, *The Anatomy of
Melancholy*, the numerous elegies, and the sermons
of the great divines. It was a time when men loved to
be subtle to plague themselves with the thought of
death. In this business Donne happened to be only
the most subtle and individual in his poetry, and the
most dramatic in his life, bringing to his own death
the tragic dignity of *Death's Duell* and the shroud.
Even as late as the notorious Rochester a profane
poet could be plagued into a last-minute repentance
by the thought of death, and the skull could mingle
with the rose in the language of a Jeremy Taylor.

But Donne wore his shroud in a way that set the
fashion; and however deeply individual his motive
for wearing it, his followers had a kindred motive in
the feeling of the time. The fashion that he set —
and it was a fashion that profoundly suited the sensibility of the age — was the Metaphysical manner of
thinking. Always fascinated and repelled by the
thought of death, he could not keep death from
mingling with and intensifying his emotions. Mr.
Courthope has traced the power of the idea that Love
is Death in some of the poems of Donne; the charnel-
house mood has been called the mood of Donne; and
many of his readers have felt themselves come closest
to his peculiar emotion in such a passage as this from
the *Second Anniversarie*:

1. *Homage to John Dryden*, p. 34.

Thinke then, my soule, that death is but a Groome,
Which brings a Taper to the outward roome,
Whence thou spiest first a little glimmering light,
And after brings it nearer to thy sight:
For such approaches doth heaven make in death.
Thinke thy selfe labouring now with broken breath,
And thinke those broken and soft Notes to bee
Division, and thy happyest Harmonie.
Thinke thee laid on thy death-bed, loose and slacke;
And thinke that, but unbinding of a packe,
To take one precious thing, thy soule from thence.[1]

Certainly this verse betrays the shroud of the seventeenth century and, though intensely individual, could have been written at no other time, and in no other way than the Metaphysical.

To find the Metaphysical shudder in its most compact form we have only to turn to the oft-quoted

A bracelet of bright haire about the bone.

No amount of repetition seems to rob this of its power. But it gains when it is coupled with those lines from *The Funerall* which begin this alliance of love and death:

Who ever comes to shroud me, do not harme
      Nor question much
That subtile wreath of haire, which crowns my arme;
The mystery, the signe you must not touch,
      For 't is my outward Soule.

This is the quality of emotion that is represented by the shroud of Donne, that is native to the sensibility

1. Grierson, *op. cit.*, i, 253–254.

of his time, and that achieves its unique expression by Metaphysical means, not least by the conceit.

Indeed the Metaphysical shudder, which we must not limit to the suggestion of death, owes much of its power to the conceit, which incorporates the sensibility of Donne's age into an expression as striking as it was contagious. Chiefly by means of the conceit the Metaphysical poets gave their thinking and feeling connections with the strange, unearthly, and terrible nebula of emotion which surrounds our life and bewilders us in the daily papers. Because of this magic we see Donne's "bracelet of bright haire about the bone" under an almost unearthly light, and shudder at the strangeness of so simple a thing. These poets were masters at releasing some plangent suggestion that communicates an effect of terror to even slight emotions. No less a talent was required in the preaching of that age, and we must remember that Donne became their great divine through the very qualities which made him their master wit.[1]

The same sensibility, if not quite the same expression, appears in Webster's famous line:

Cover her face; mine eyes dazzle; she died young. [2]

The taste for the horrible which the Jacobean drama reveals is only another facet of the sensibility whose Metaphysical shudder I am trying to define. Mr. T. S. Eliot has caught this shudder while describing

1. See Simpson, *Prose Works of John Donne*, pp. 234 ff.
2. Regard this in the light of two other flashes:
    As lightning, or a Tapers light,
    Thine eyes, and not thy noise wak'd mee. — Donne.
"There is a part of divinity that dazzles; if we look too long on it, we may well lose our sight." — Lancelot Andrewes.

the sensibility of Webster and Donne in *Whispers of Immortality*:

> Webster was much possessed by death
> And saw the skull beneath the skin;
> And breastless creatures under ground
> Leaned backward with a lipless grin.
>
> Daffodil bulbs instead of balls
> Stared from the sockets of the eyes!
> He knew that thought clings round dead limbs
> Tightening its lusts and luxuries.

Nothing could more accurately describe this sensibility, and nothing could more convincingly relate this shudder to its very means of expression, for the verse itself is Metaphysical. But let us turn to Donne's contemporaries.

All the true Metaphysical poets seem to have the ability, modified by their native talent, to incorporate this Metaphysical shudder into their verse, and invariably by means of the very things which make their verse Metaphysical. Let me illustrate this peculiar quality of emotion in a number of them. First in Herbert, whose nature was much less intense than Donne's:

> Onely a sweet and vertuous soul,
> Like season'd timber, never gives;
> But though the whole world turn to coal,
>   Then chiefly lives.[1]

I confess I do not get the sense of the ludicrous which many critics feel in this, though I might if I stopped with the "season'd timber"; rather, I am brought

1. *Vertue.*

up with a jar at the tremendous contrast of "though the whole world turn to coal." This gives the thought a connection with the terrible nebula of emotion which constitutes the Metaphysical surprise and which Pascal felt in the terror of the infinite. Compare the lines from *Church-Monuments*:

> thou mayst know
> That flesh is but the glasse which holds the dust
> That measures all our time; which also shall
> Be crumbled into dust.

Here we have an example of the charnel-house mood of Donne.

Crashaw, with the modification of his more erotic mind, could also achieve this shudder:

> Thus
> When These thy Deaths, so numerous,
> Shall all at last dy into one,
> And melt thy Soul's sweet mansion;
> Like a soft lump of incense, hasted
> By too hott a fire, & wasted
> Into perfuming clouds, so fast
> Shalt thou exhale to Heaun at last
> In a resolving Sigh, and then
> O what? Ask not the Tongues of men.[1]

Does this conceit not give the emotion of death that peculiar Metaphysical strangeness? Or this from Vaughan?

> Think then, that in this bed
> There sleep the Reliques of as proud a head
> As stern and subtill as your own.[2]

1. *Hymn to Saint Teresa*, Martin, *The Poems of Richard Crashaw*, p. 320.
2. *The Charnel-house*, Martin, *The Works of Henry Vaughan*, i, 42.

Or if you would feel it in something less like an echo
of Donne and more like Vaughan, read this:

> If a star were confin'd into a Tomb
>   Her captive flames must needs burn there;
> But when the hand that lockt her up, gives room,
>   She'l shine through all the sphaere.[1]

If these poets continually sought novelty, as Dr.
Johnson charged, their search at least had the merit
of frequently communicating the peculiar shudder
with which they "saw the skull beneath the skin,"
caught their emotions in the light of a Metaphysical
connection, or knew "the fever of the bone."

In Lord Herbert we find another variation of the
same shudder, communicated in a conceit which
makes his emotion at once mysterious and precise:

> Must I then see, alas! eternal night
>   Sitting upon those fairest eyes,
> And closing all those beams, which once did rise
>   So radiant and bright,
> That light and heat in them to us did prove
>   Knowledge and Love?[2]

And still there is Benlowes:

> Death's serjeant soon thy courted Helens must
>   Attach, whose eyes, now orbs of lust,
> The worms shall feed on, till they crumble into dust.[3]

But in this passage from Bishop King we feel more of

---

1. *Ascension-Hymn, ibid.,* ii, 484.
2. *Elegy over a Tomb.*
3. Saintsbury, *op. cit.,* i, 427.

the fierce intensity of Donne and his Metaphysical shudder:

> But the black Map of death and discontent
> Behind that Adamantine firmament,
> That luckless figure which like Calvary
> Stands strew'd and coppy'd out in skuls, is I:
> Whose life your absence clouds, and makes my time
> Move blindfold in the dark ecliptick line.[1]

Even Marvell, whose emotions we are inclined at times to call slight, knew "the fever of the bone" and could communicate the shudder with his Metaphysical surprise:

> But at my back I alwaies hear
> Times winged Charriot hurrying near:
> And yonder all before us lye
> Desarts of vast Eternity . . .
> The Grave's a fine and private place,
> But none I think do there embrace.[2]

The wit in the last line is an indication of how one of these poets could further qualify his emotion with levity.

And so we see how Donne and his shroud, individual but kin to the sensibility of his age, represent a particular way of thinking and feeling, and receive unique expression in the Metaphysical shudder. We could scarcely ask for better evidence that there is a quality of emotion peculiar to the Metaphysical mode of thought than the anthology of quotations

---

1. *An Acknowledgment.*
2. *To his Coy Mistress,* Margoliouth, *The Poems and Letters of Andrew Marvell,* i, 26.

which I have given. Proof can only be made complete by reading the poets themselves. Donne and his shroud, Donne and his age, meet in such a line as

And thou like Adamant draw mine iron heart.[1]

Emotion like this he taught his followers to express after him. To them we may now direct our attention.

1. *Holy Sonnets*, I.

V. THE SACRED LINE

GEORGE HERBERT

FIRST among the Carolines to follow Donne in religious verse was George Herbert. Of all the Metaphysicals, Herbert is in some ways most like Donne. It is very difficult to form any opinion of his native talent before it was touched by the Donne influence; for his earliest English poems, the *Two Sonnets* to his mother, already bear the marks of Donne. Perhaps the most fruitful way of discovering what Herbert was apart from the Donne influence is to see how he modified that influence. While there is evidence in Palmer's critical edition of Herbert to show that the direct Donne bias grew relatively less as Herbert approached poetic maturity, the fact that this influence did not disappear suggests how congenial the Metaphysical method was to Herbert and how like, at bottom, he was to Donne.

The second *Jordan* tells us that when Herbert took his resolve to give himself to devotional verse, he consciously sought to improve his technique for that service. The change is certainly in the direction of Donne as Herbert describes it:

When first my lines of heav'nly joyes made mention,
   Such was their lustre, they did so excell,
That I sought out quaint words and trim invention;

My thoughts began to burnish, sprout, and swell,
Curling with metaphors a plain intention,
    Decking the sense as if it were to sell.

Although this early adoption of the Metaphysical
method complicates his native talent, we may trust
our general impression and his hint that it was nearer
"a plain intention" than it was to the subtlety of
Donne. In contrast to Donne, *The Temple* reveals a
poet who has a spontaneous sincerity which permits
a more direct approach to God, and a secure faith
which, despite his sense of sin, brings him to ac-
quiescence within the quiet shadow of the Church.
His *Affliction* is not the sceptical agony of a Donne,
but the lament of a temperate Job; he lacks the gnaw-
ing remorse and the lacerating passion of Donne.
Herbert is more at ease in Zion. And greater distance
seems to separate God from Donne, because a more
complex mind enters into his communion, with the
result that he seems to be in profounder distress and
on less personal relations. The more intellectual sophistication of Donne withheld the simple sincerity
that made moralizing possible and effective in Herbert.

Herbert's poetry was served by a fine and delicate
sensibility, which by the side of Donne's has something dainty about it, something that reminds one of
Herrick or of Cavalier flowers. Walton says that in
The Odour Herbert

seems to rejoice in the thoughts of that word Jesus, and
say, that the adding these words, my master, to it, and the

often repetition of them seemed to perfume his mind, and leave an Oriental fragrancy in his very breath.[1]

This is a valuable commentary on the sensuous thinking of Herbert. Though his sensibility was capable of producing weeds and even ranker growths, it naturally was like his

> Sweet spring, full of sweet dayes and roses,
> A box where sweets compacted lie;[2]

which might be emptied into his metaphors or forsaken for the homelier expressions of chaster seasons. In a similar way one feels that Herbert's imagination is less massive and less robust than Donne's; that it realizes itself best in the smaller conceptions of *The Pulley*, *The Windows*, *The Collar*, or *Vertue*; and that it has a certain affinity for neat designs and comfortable limits.

The same fastidiousness of sensibility and imagination appears in his scrupulous concern for art, which Palmer has demonstrated in his edition of Herbert, where he is shown to be "an intentional, long-continued, and ever-revising workman." Palmer also shows that Herbert is careful of the regularity of his metre, though not at the expense of variety of music, and that he experiments unceasingly with metrical form. The passage which I quoted from the second *Jordan* shows that Herbert was a conscious craftsman and likely to be interested in the technique of his fellow poets.

1. Walton's *Lives* (Morley's Universal Library), pp. 253–254.
2. *Vertue.*

The most influential poet of the time, Donne, was a friend of the Herberts while George Herbert was still in his 'teens. This friendship must have begun shortly before 1607, for Walton's *Life of Herbert* contains a letter of gratitude from Donne to Lady Herbert which was addressed in that year. The most significant thing in this letter for us is the information that Donne accompanied the letter with some holy hymns and sonnets. Now if we turn to the poem *Praise*, one of Herbert's earliest English poems according to Palmer, we shall find that, along with other reminders of Donne, the refrain of this poem is that of the *Hymn to God the Father*.[1] Besides making it certain that the dating of one of these poems is wrong, so striking an example of influence makes us wonder how much those holy hymns and sonnets had to do with Herbert's resolve to sing the praises of God, especially since his Latin poems are without the devotional spirit,[2] and since *Praise* shows that divine aid was now a necessity of his muse. Herbert's lines to Donne tell us that he thought of Donne as a religious poet or preacher, and that this was the side of Donne which appealed to him.

At least, the influence of Donne was strong enough to make a poet who echoed the style of no other poet quote entire lines from him, parody one of his *Songs*, or one apparently his, and otherwise imitate him.[3]

1. See G. H. Palmer, *English Works of George Herbert*, ii, 94.
2. *Ibid.*, i, 103.
3. *Ibid.*, p. 71. On the imitation see Palmer for lines in *Mortification*, *Parodie* (? Donne's *Song*), *Church-Porch*, other close echoes, the device of a Corona of divine sonnets in *Sinnes Rounde*, etc.

In *Church-Monuments* the sensibility which Donne made available for poetry moulds one of Herbert's finest poems, and gives an eloquent witness to the way in which Donne modified the sensibility of his time:

> While that my soul repairs to her devotion,
>   Here I intombe my flesh, that it betimes
>   May take acquaintance of this heap of dust,
> To which the blast of death's incessant motion,
>   Fed with the exhalation of our crimes,
>   Drives all at last. Therefore I gladly trust
>
> My bodie to this school, that it may learn
>   To spell his elements, and finde his birth
>   Written in dustie heraldrie and lines
> Which dissolution sure doth best discern,
>   Comparing dust with dust, and earth with earth.

These lines are enough to show a kind of poetry in Herbert that, while still his own, is yet so thoroughly Donnean as to distinguish it rather sharply from the poems his name usually calls to mind. In connection with the manner of Herbert's imitation, we shall have to examine Palmer's claim for his originality: "He devised the religious love-lyric, and he introduced structure into the short poem." [1]

The manner in which Herbert paid homage to Donne was to take over the chief features of the Metaphysical method and to follow his master in developing religious verse. Palmer's claim that Herbert devised the religious love lyric cannot be allowed to

1. *Ibid.*, p. 87.

stand as an unequivocal statement; in fact, Palmer's own candor in his chapter on "The Religious Poetry" causes him to make various conflicting statements while coming to this conclusion. Donne troubles him most, and the way he gets round Donne is by asserting that while his *Holy Sonnets* show "Herbert's own deep communing with God" they are too intellectual to be genuinely devout.[1] The saving word in Palmer's claim is *love*, for there is something of the Petrarchian lover in Herbert's devotional verse which we do not get in the troubled accents of Donne's profound distress. The sense of religious fear which kept Donne from achieving this personal love was not strong enough in Herbert to keep him from fulfilling his resolve to devote a lover's praise to his God. However, it seems to me mere quibbling to say that Donne's *Holy Sonnets* do not fulfill the requirements of Palmer's definition of the religious lyric: "The religious lyric is a cry of the individual heart to God." [2] Consequently, I believe that justice requires us to say that Herbert really carried on the strangely personal religious poetry of Donne, and achieved in it an emotional simplicity and a sacred love that are perhaps more appropriate to the best devotional verse.

The second part of Palmer's claim, that Herbert introduced structure into the short poem, seems to me equally a part of the influence of Donne. The "articulated structure" which Palmer claims Herbert vindicated as a working factor in poetry, in spite

1. *Op. cit.*, i, 89 and 97.
2. *Ibid.*, p. 94.

of its sporadic appearance before,[1] is nothing but the rational evolution that I have shown in Donne, whose lyric is certainly as articulated as anything Herbert ever wrote. Palmer's test for this structure,[2] which Jonson's *"Drinke to me only with thine eyes"* fails to survive, whether part with part has any private amity, is certainly a test made for the author of *The Dreame*, *The Extasie*, or *The Relique*. The almost syllogistic relation of thought to thought, stanza to stanza, in Donne's verse is one of his most striking characteristics and one of the surest signs of the intellectual cast of his poetry. I do not wish to deny the structure which Herbert so evidently has, but merely to point out the priority of Donne in this respect. However, there is a difference in their structure worth noting: the articulation of Herbert's thought, because of the smaller character of his mind (which conforms to his sensibility and imagination), is less complex and more in accord with the trim invention which he sought and found congenial to his talent.

The more obvious features of the Metaphysical method as it was taken over by Herbert remain to be considered. Of course he employed the conceit which Donne had developed as the agent of wit and of powerful imaginative surprise. Of this Metaphysical

1. Notably in the sonnet, where articulated structure is too consistently present to be regarded as sporadic. In fact, it is probable that such structure spread from the sonnet to the other lyric forms. The great period of English sonnet-writing coincides with the probable years of Donne's *Songs and Sonets*, in which the form of the sonnet has broken down and its structure has spread to the song. There, however, it has become even more syllogistic than it was in the sonnet.

2. *Op. cit.*, i, 139–140.

surprise, which seems to me one of the glories of this
poetry, there is a splendid example in Herbert's
charming poem, *Vertue*; an example that almost earns
a place beside the famous one in Marvell's *Coy Mistress.* You remember how *Vertue* begins with the

> Sweet day, so cool, so calm, so bright,

and goes on to the Spring,

> A box where sweets compacted lie;

to end with the following stanza,

> Onely a sweet and vertuous soul,
> Like season'd timber, never gives;
> But though the whole world turn to coal,
>   Then chiefly lives.

What a sudden influx of stupendous and chilling
thought there is in that last line but one! This is
the sort of thought and emotion which provoked
Marvell's

> But at my back I alwaies hear
> Times winged Charriot hurrying near:

the way of thinking and feeling which is represented
by the conceit, and which makes one pause before
declaring the conceit an affectation of seventeenth-
century poetry. It seems to me much safer to ask
ourselves when the conceit fails — as it often does,
or the critics would not be so savagely against it —
what makes it fail?

An excellent test for the conceit is given by Palmer
in this question: "Does it by thought exclude feel-

ing, or does it through thought embody feeling in some new, individual, and subtle way?" [1] When a feelingless conceit falsifies the emotional sequence of a poem, we sense the emotional duplicity which we call insincerity and affectation. The packed phrases that strike us as conceits in the Metaphysical poets are not in themselves bad, but they run the added dangers that always attend the daring use of language in the effort to force it into meaning. Let me set down two notorious examples and tempt the critics. First, one from *Hamlet* at the time of Ophelia's drowning:

> Too much of water hast thou, poor Ophelia,
> And therefore I forbid my tears.

Then this one from Herbert's *Dawning*:

> Christ left his grave-clothes that we might, when grief
> Draws tears or bloud, not want an handkerchief.

Certainly this gives my opponents a fair mark; but can they accuse Herbert of more emotional duplicity than Shakspere falls into? Incidentally, this comparison shows how much more thoughtful the Metaphysical conceit is in contrast to the Elizabethan conceit. I do not contend that the Metaphysical poets did not often fail in their use of conceits, any more than I should care to defend Shakspere's universal success with his figures; but I do contend that the conceit should be reprimanded by the usual canons of poetic taste and not by wholesale dismissal as the affectation of a renegade century.

1. *Op. cit.*, i, 161.

The lines from the second *Jordan* which I have already quoted tell us how Herbert took up the Metaphysical manner when he began to write devotional verse, how he sought out "quaint words and trim invention," and how his thoughts began to "curl with metaphors a plain intention." His avowal is supported by our impression of his verse; for the Metaphysical influence seems to have carried him toward complexity until he could assert,

> As flames do work and winde when they ascend,
>   So did I weave my self into the sense.

While the conclusion to this stanza of the second *Jordan* shows that he probably had moments when he doubted the wisdom of such complexity, we may question whether he could have woven himself into the sense of his devotional verse, with the same highly original results, if he had not followed the lead of Donne. Without the Metaphysical method, the lyrics which represent Herbert in the anthologies would lose all their savor and much of their power to trace the original contours of his religious experience; in truth, it is nearly impossible to think of poems like *The Windows* or *The Pulley* without the conceit. But the implication of a conceit by means of the title given to a poem is a device peculiar to Herbert.

Although there is something in the way Herbert's mind associated ideas and linked images that lent itself naturally to the manner of Donne, there is at the same time less complexity in his mind, in the association of his ideas, and in the sequence of his images. But Palmer finds him more difficult than Donne, and says that "it costs him but a slight change of phrase to turn one of Donne's love-songs into one of his own kind." Slight, but how far-reaching! For *A Parodie* simplifies the song *Soules joy now I am gone*, by reducing the number of associated ideas and by making the sequence of images more homogeneous. If this song belongs to the Earl of Pembroke, one of Donne's circle, and not to Donne, as Grierson argues, it is at least so like Donne in most ways that it offers an instructive contact between Herbert and the Metaphysical tradition. If Herbert is more difficult than Donne, it is not because his mind is more complex. Without the Metaphysical influence Herbert would still be a poet, but not the poet of *Vertue, The Collar,* or *Church-Monuments.*

In yet other ways Herbert is indebted to Donne. Palmer has remarked that classical allusions are plentiful in Herbert's Latin poems and very scarce in his English poems, hardly more than a half-dozen in the whole *Temple;* and that this is the more striking because his education inclined him to accept them.[1] Remembering how this disdain for classical allusions marks Donne's revolt against Elizabethan tradition, and how it distinguished him for the Metaphysicals, we must attribute this sudden change in Herbert to the Donne tradition which he accepted in his devotional verse. The quaint words which he has confessed, and which have often been pointed out in him,

1. *Op. cit.,* i, 166.

are similar to the homely and learned words we meet in Donne, with the difference that Herbert's quaint words are more exactly simple. Colloquial directness is likewise to be found in his lines. But Herbert, when compared to Donne, lacks something in weight and extent of learning; and this limitation probably explains why he succeeds in being more concrete than Donne, why he is able to express almost everything by imagery. This ability is the sensuous apprehension of thought which I have tried to analyze in Donne and to define as something peculiar to the Metaphysical way of thinking and feeling.

While it is true to say that Herbert applied the Metaphysical method to the religious lyric, the whole truth demands that the stress be somewhat differently placed, for this statement neglects the beginning which Donne made. Rather than give Herbert the emphasis of a pioneer, it is a little more exact to say that Herbert simply carried on the sacred side of the Donne tradition and developed it in certain ways. The line of development is sufficiently defined when we say that Herbert, by accenting love and pure simplicity of language and heart, but not neglecting psychological experience, converted Donne's religious lyric into the finest devotional verse of the seventeenth century. While Herbert thus stems from Donne, it is through *The Temple* that the religious side of Donne passed to other poets who reflected his manner of praise even when they forgot his name.

RICHARD CRASHAW

The sacred line continues in Richard Crashaw. A great admirer of Herbert, Crashaw shows his admiration by following *The Temple* with *Steps to the Temple*. The anonymous preface contains these words: "Here's Herbert's second, but equall, who hath retriv'd Poetry of late, and return'd it up to its Primitive use; Let it bound back to heaven gates, whence it came." With the suggestion that here is Donne's third, we may let his poetry bound back to the only begetter of the Metaphysical line.

Though Italian influence came early to Crashaw, the influence of Herbert and Donne was earlier and stronger. The friendship of Nicholas Ferrar established a living connection between Crashaw and the work of Herbert. Such early poems as those on the death of Mr. Herrys, which belong to 1631, show that while Crashaw's luxurious temperament is already present, it is restrained by a more masculine spirit than his later poems reveal.[1] The sombre, virile, and tough conceit and texture of Donne are perhaps even more apparent in such poems as *Vpon Bishop* Andrewes *his Picture*, *On the Frontispiece of* Isaacsons *Chronologie*, or *In praise of* Lessius, all published before 1635. And the elegy *Vpon Mr.* Staninough's *Death*, written in 1635, is much more like Donne than like the poetry we associate with Crashaw, and nowhere more than in its images. To this list of

---

1. For dates see L. C. Martin, *The Poems of Richard Crashaw*, pp. lxxxvi–xcii.

Donnean poems we could add others; for instance, the one *On a Treatise of Charity*, in which there is an echo of Herbert's *Church Floore* in the idea that "marbles weep." Professor Martin has already noted parallels to Donne in the poem on Lessius and in *The Weeper*, which is chiefly Italian in spirit and manner.[1] These early poems are certainly closer to Herbert's *Church-Monuments* in mood and temper than they are to the Teresa poems.

By his own avowal Crashaw carries us back to Herbert, through whom the religious side of the Donne tradition descended, and from whom Crashaw differs in ways that are his own and in ways that are Donne's. Compared with one another, Crashaw represents more of Donne's ecstasy, and Herbert more of his reason. What is peculiar to Crashaw himself may be suggested if we will imagine the Gentlewoman to whom he sent his poem *On Master* George Herberts *booke* putting down that book and picking up Mr. Crashaw's *Carmen Deo Nostro* with the desire

> To flutter in the balmy aire
> Of your well perfumed prayer.[2]

For Crashaw has a voluptuous mysticism that suggests a mixture of two powerful qualities of Donne's mind in a feminine way that is alien to Donne's masculine sensuality and to Herbert's chaste love. After the fashion of his cherished Saint Teresa, Cra-

1. See Commentary in the Martin edition of Crashaw.
2. Martin, *op. cit.*, p. 130.

shaw partly substituted divine love for human love, not without some confusion, in his need to express the luxury of his senses. In the early poems his luxurious vein, though present, was undeveloped. Very soon, however, Italian influence turned this vein into the channel of jewelled conceits and sensuous sighs; later, Jesuit literature opened the way to erotic mysticism.

Unlike Herbert, Crashaw represents both the sacred and the profane side of Donne's genius, subtly in the voluptuous mysticism we have just noticed and obviously in his authorship of both religious and amatory verses. But his poetry has lost the searching introspection and anxious personality which distinguishes that of Herbert, and even more that of Donne. This loss has resulted in a poetry of religious states more outward than intimate in its passion for heavenly objects: witness the *Hymn to Saint Teresa*, inspired by the 1642 translation of the biography, *The Flaming Hart or the Life of the Glorious S. Teresa.* Gone, too, is most of the analysis of a Herbert or a Donne. Instead of analyzing his own religious evolution, Crashaw is concerned to represent mystical states and to employ his meagre analysis in describing the complex emotions which compose these religious moods. *The Flaming Heart* shows just such a mood, as well as the artistic destiny of such moods, in the lines:

> O sweet incendiary! shew here thy art,
> Upon this carcasse of a hard, cold, hart,[1]

1. *Ibid.*, p. 326, ll. 85–86.

which is anything but cold when it becomes the
"love-slain witness" of a mystical state. However,
the artistic destiny of such moods in Crashaw is seldom as personal as this. Being less analytical, the
emotions of Crashaw lack the precise outline of the
emotions of Herbert and Donne. The greater influence of the musical sensibility — response to
hearing, smell, and taste — in Crashaw doubtless explains some of the vague mingling of emotion and
emotion which strikes us as we come to him from
Herbert and Donne.

Though Crashaw thus modified the religious love
lyric which Herbert developed from Donne's beginning, he did not take over the trim structure of Herbert or the rational structure of Donne. His poems
lack that private amity which is so subtle in Donne
and so neat in Herbert; in fact, such poems as *The
Weeper* and *Wishes* have only the structure that is
given by the string in a rosary. Not even his most
perfect poem, the *Hymn to Saint Teresa*, has more
structure than emotion breaking upon emotion or the
ecstasy of Saint Teresa, which here so strangely resembles the love-death of an Iseult. At Crashaw's
hands the structure of Herbert died "a death more
mysticall and high" than was to be its fate in later
times. And yet the structure of his sentences is often
more complex than that of Herbert, though generally
simpler than Donne's; but, none the less, it goes with
more lyric flow, because the burden of thought is not
so great as to steal from grace for the sake of nervy
strength.

Crashaw probably stood in as much danger of the fatal facility which reduces *sense* to a vague blur as Swinburne, but he never became a victim of the cult of imprecision, largely I think because of the analytic strain which the conceit induces. How close he could come to the school in which the *sound* and not the *sense* appears to give the meaning, even while persuading a lady to resolution in religion, may be heard in these lines *To the Countesse of Denbigh*:

> Ah linger not, lou'd soul! a slow
> And late consent was a long no,
> Who grants at last, long time tryd
> And did his best to haue deny'd.
> What magick bolts, what mystick Barres
> Maintain the will in these strange warres!

This melodious magic seems to blur all but its own music; but the very next lines begin to weave a thoughtful conceit that casts a penetrating light over what we have just read, opens a window upon the soul, and introduces the nervy strength of Donne into the mystic flow of the verse:

> What fatall, yet fantastick, bands
> Keep The free Heart from it's own hands!
> So when the year takes cold, we see
> Poor waters their owne prisoners be.
> Fetter'd, & lockt vp fast they ly
> In a sad selfe-captiuity.
> The' astonisht nymphs their flood's strange fate deplore,
> To see themselues their own seuerer shore.[1]

How concrete this figure renders a thought very dif-

1. Martin, *op. cit.*, p. 237.

ficult to express directly, and how much more precise the articulation of thought becomes! Incidentally, this is the Radical image of Donne, like the image of death and the unbinding of a pack, with a minor term of little imaginative value compelled into a powerful metaphorical relation which has a definite effect upon the music. The sinewy thought in this conceit stamps it as belonging to the manner of Donne and not to the Italian concettist style for which Crashaw may in part be claimed; this conceit becomes a structural decoration of the thought, without which the feeling would lack precision.

The strong influence of Italian and Jesuit literature turned Crashaw into the most baroque of the English Metaphysicals, but such influence does not account for passages like the one just examined. In this European baroque quality Crashaw is most sharply distinguished from Donne, who, though doubtless influenced by Spanish literature, was intensely English and intensely himself. But if the conceit in Crashaw is often merely ingeniously ornamental, which it almost never is in Donne, the toughly analytic and structural conceit of Donne is common enough in him to warrant his inclusion in the Donne tradition, and to justify our believing that, had Donne never been, such a passage as the one last quoted would not have been written.

This conclusion is supported by the poem *To the Countesse of Denbigh* and by certain general facts. Since this poem is the closest in texture of any of Crashaw's, and also a work of mature genius, it belongs with the Teresa poems and the *Answer for Hope* rather than with *The Weeper* or *The Teare*, poems in which the Italian influence is predominant. It is a late poem, having been printed first in 1652; and it reveals the nature of Crashaw's mature talent, whose direction is more fully revealed in the revision of the poem in 1653. This direction is one of more complex texture, which first appears in the *Answer for Hope* and is remote from the ingenuity of the Italian verses. In the *Answer for Hope*, probably written after the Italian verses and before the Teresa poems, Crashaw is matching Cowley stanza for stanza. When connected with Crashaw's admiration for Cowley, this fact is very significant: it means the reassertion of the Donne tradition in Crashaw. By this time the Italian influence had lost its force in him; the jewelled conceits and ingenious ornament of *The Weeper* could no longer support his emotions, which were growing more complex and rapid in their alterations and antitheses. Crashaw was getting more concerned for the essence of things; hence his poetry began to take on the quality represented by Herbert's *Quidditie* and satirized by Butler in the lines,

> He knew *what's what*, and that's as high
> As *Metaphysick* wit can fly.[1]

This quality was of course immensely important in the poetry of Donne, and is indeed the very genius of Cowley's poem *Against Hope*.

1. Grierson, *Metaphysical Poetry*, p. 214.

We have but to look at the verse in which Crashaw matched Cowley to see the reassertion of the Donne tradition in Crashaw. Let us look at the beginning of the poem as it was first printed:

Cowley

Hope, whose weake being ruin'd is
Alike, if it succeed, and if it misse.
Whom Ill, and Good doth equally confound,
And both the hornes of Fates dilemma wound.
    Vaine shadow! that doth vanish quite
    Both at full noone, and perfect night.
    The Fates have not a possibility
        Of blessing thee.
If things then from their ends wee happy call,
'T is hope is the most hopelesse thing of all.

Crashaw

Deare Hope! Earths dowry, and Heavens debt,
The entity of things that are not yet.
Subt'lest, but surest being! Thou by whom
Our Nothing hath a definition.
    Faire cloud of fire, both shade, and light,
    Our life in death, our day in night.
    Fates cannot find out a capacity
        Of hurting thee.
From thee their thinne dilemma with blunt horne
Shrinkes, like the sick Moone at the wholsome morne.[1]

This is the Crashaw whom we have already seen in the lines to the Countess of Denbigh, the mature Crashaw; and this is the direction in which his talent developed after the Italian influence; but not from

1. Martin, *op. cit.*, p. 143.

it, for this direction is within the Donne tradition. Here Crashaw shares with Cowley the analysis and close thinking which derive from Donne. The revised form of this poem gives additional emphasis to these qualities, and because of its complex texture, takes its place among the mature works of Crashaw. His lines *Upon two greene Apricokes sent to* Cowley *by Sir* Crashaw support the theory that the Donne influence on Crashaw was renewed through Cowley, and affirm the conclusion that Italian influence cannot account for Crashaw's mature genius.

The *Letter to the Countess of Denbigh*, the last version of this poem and Crashaw's last poem, is closer to Donne in its complex metaphorical utterance than any other poem Crashaw wrote. Notwithstanding the frequent use of the ornamental conceit — the Italian sort — in Crashaw, as in *Wishes* and *The Weeper*, the characteristic effects of the structural conceit of Donne are found in the better poems of Crashaw. If we turn to the *Hymn to Saint Teresa*, we shall find Donne's conceit and his sensuous thinking, but combined with Crashaw's voluptuous mysticism, giving a sensuous rendering for a state of ecstasy. Donne's "large draughts of intellectual day" are unmistakable in the following lines:

> Thus
> When These thy Deaths, so numerous,
> Shall all at last dy into one,
> And melt thy Soul's sweet mansion;
> Like a soft lump of incense, hasted
> By too hott a fire, & wasted

Into perfuming clouds, so fast
Shalt thou exhale to Heaun at last
In a resoluing Sigh, and then
O what? ask not the Tongues of men.[1]

It is only because of Donne's conquest of mystical expression that "the Tongues of men" do not fail Crashaw sooner. The conceit here does for the sweet incendiary what it does for Donne in *The Extasie*: it chains analysis to emotion; and keeping the flame of Crashaw's lyric feeling within limits, it saves him from the fireworks of colored words which carried Swinburne away. The more remarkable does this appear when one reflects that his poetic temptations were similar to those of Swinburne, even to a fondness for words like *flame*, *white*, *silver*, *purple*, and *gold*. Perhaps the chief reason that Crashaw's lyric fluency did not release more words is that the Donne conceit induces an analytic strain which is astringent in its effect.

Not less striking, it seems to me, is the evidence of Donne in that passage of *The Flaming Heart* which we give the highest praise, the part beginning "O sweet incendiary!" [2] This part was added to the last version of the poem as it appeared in 1652, and hence represents the mature genius of Crashaw. Up to this passage of the poem Crashaw has been using the conceit as an outlet for his voluptuous mysticism; then suddenly his imagination takes fire at the thought of Saint Teresa's relation to him, and at once the con-

1. Martin, *op. cit*, p. 320.
2. *Ibid.*, pp. 326–327.

ceit becomes a structural part of his emotion, the thought tightens, becoming subtlest at the end, and the emotion grows tense, breaking into invocation; and the whole passage admits a note of analysis into its highest lyric reach. Although I would not press the influence in this passage of the "large draughts of intellectual day" which came from Donne, it is not to be lightly disregarded, especially when the second stanza of *Loves Deitie* begins to stir in our memory as we read

> Loue's passiues are his actiu'st part.
> The wounded is the wounding heart.[1]

Just after these lines, even in the early version, Crashaw's imagination begins to kindle. The suggestion of influence grows stronger when we observe that before these lines the "happy fire-works" of Crashaw are for the most part the pretty confectionery conceits of the Italians, but afterward they become the homelier conceit of Donne, at the same time losing their voluptuous color and their employment as prettification. In brief, the conceit after the Donne manner brings an intellectual element which fetters and locks up fast in a powerful precision the subtle and mystical emotions of Crashaw, at the same time releasing their affective power, like a magnifying glass, by bringing them to a focus. Once more we discover that the conceit, so often regarded as merely a wilful ingenuity, represents a particular way of thinking and feeling.

1. *Ibid.*, p. 326.

The faults of taste with which Crashaw's conceit must be charged, notably in *The Weeper*, derive from what we may call his Italian manner of using this figure, the decorative way rather than the structural way of Donne, although there are faults on the other side too. The Donne side of Crashaw's inheritance includes a use of paradox, which we passed over in Herbert because it is nothing like so prevalent. This appears characteristically in *Loves Horoscope*, where it is part of the texture of the poem — a poem, by the way, which achieves structural unity unusual in Crashaw, because its form is imposed upon it by the extended conceit which it develops.[1] In this poem we can see very clearly what the Donne influence, working through Herbert or directly, meant for Crashaw: it introduced fundamental brain work into the color, ardor, and harmony of his lyric talent. Without this influence, his lines on *The Weeper* would still be what they are, but his *Hymn to Saint Teresa* would not be the poem it is. If Crashaw, rather neglecting the reason of Donne, carries the ecstasy to its highest pitch, the analysis of Donne is at least present enough in his best poems to keep him from floating off into the mystical inane or falling into ornamental absurdities. This is granting Crashaw more success than many are inclined to give him; but it is not, I believe, giving the Donne tradition more credit than it deserves for its astringent effect upon Crashaw's poetry.

1. The extended conceit is also to be found in Petrarch, where it plays a similar but not quite Donnean part.

It is as a poet of rhapsodical passages that Crashaw excels, and yet he was a conscious artist, as his practice of revision shows. With qualities that might have made him a Swinburne, even to the decadent use of *white*, he managed, through his Metaphysical inheritance, to give his best poetic rhapsody the firm score which will support the most ecstatic flight and define the most mystical thought. Yet he is a true representative of the European baroque poet, contrasting with Donne therein; for Crashaw is the most European poet in the sacred line of the Metaphysicals, as Marvell is in the profane line. And again like Marvell, he has, on his side of the tradition, the greatest perfection of language and the highest command of lyric music. But Crashaw's ability to make his mysticism at least as tangible as incense is an ability which he shares with Donne.

HENRY VAUGHAN

In Henry Vaughan mysticism turns to Nature and finds there its Metaphysical imagery and its inspiration. Through his sympathy with Nature the conceit annexes another great domain of symbolism, for Vaughan made Nature his special province and explored its riches with peculiar insight. Here he is far from Crashaw, whose mysticism is concerned with the sensuous and learned symbols of the Catholic Church and is more likely to feel the presence of God in burning incense than in a rushing wind. Although a true mystic, Vaughan does not look to Crashaw for poetic guidance, but first to Donne and later to Herbert. When he turns to Herbert it is not to give up the Donne manner but to follow paths that lead only to God, regretting, like Donne, his early love lyrics, inoffensive as they are.

In his preface to *Silex Scintillans* Vaughan marks this turning with the statement:

> The first, that with any effectual success attempted a *diversion* of this foul and overflowing *stream*, was the blessed man, Mr. *George Herbert*, whose holy *life* and *verse* gained many pious *Converts*, (of whom I am the least) and gave the first check to a most flourishing and admired *wit* of his time.[1]

For this "admired *wit*," Vaughan's editors have suggested several contemporaries of Herbert; but this seems to me unnecessary, since Vaughan's remarks show that he is using *wit* as a general term, and not to designate a person. The next words of the text, "After him followed diverse," may be the cause of the misinterpretation; but close reading of the whole passage will show that the masculine pronouns refer to Herbert and not to an unknown wit, and that Vaughan is talking about "a *good* wit in a *bad* subject," and the reverse, throughout the whole preface. The foul and overflowing stream, to which Vaughan felt he had contributed, came from a most flourishing and admired wit which was the style in verse, and which, since it came from Donne, Vaughan was not to escape by turning to Herbert. In all probability this is only another expression of the sentiment which

1. L. C. Martin, *The Works of Henry Vaughan*, ii, 391.

we found in the preface to *Steps to the Temple*, the sentiment of retrieving poetry for religious purposes. It is curious that both Crashaw and Vaughan seem unaware of what Carew and others were aware of, that Donne was the true God's priest as well as Apollo's. No doubt this is to be explained by Herbert's peculiar appeal as a poet in the Donne tradition who was purely a religious poet. The presence of Herbert allowed poets who revolted from the profane side of Donne, which obscured his religious side for them, to turn to a disciple of his religious side who wrote in the same manner.

Vaughan's first poems, published in 1646, were addressed "To all Ingenious Lovers of Poesie" and were apparently for the most part inspired by Donne's love lyrics, to which they pay the homage of imitation. Reading them, we find ourselves agreeing with his prefatory words: *"the fire at highest is but* Platonick."[1] The quiet of the countryside is too much in Vaughan's blood for him to achieve the throbbing urban passion of Donne or even the lesser agitation of a man like Crashaw. Compared with the Metaphysicals we have considered, Vaughan's emotion seems more solitary and more unsocial, in the sense of lacking contacts with a society.

In these early poems Donne's direct influence is easy to discover; it has been pointed out by various critics. Such lines as these betray it: in *To Amoret gone from him*,

Those things that element their love,[2]

1. *Ibid.*, i, 2.   2. *Ibid.*, p. 8.

and in *An Elegy*,

> In them the Metempsuchosis of Love;[1]

while such a line as this in *Upon the Priorie Grove*,

> Shall these greene curles bring to decay,[2]

points in the direction of Marvell. But most obviously the influence appears in *To* Amoret, *of the difference 'twixt him, and other Lovers, and what true Love is.* In *A Valediction: forbidding mourning* Donne had written:

> Dull sublunary lovers love
> (Whose soule is sense) cannot admit
> Absence, because it doth remove
> Those things which elemented it.
>
> But we by a love, so much refin'd,
> That our selves know not what it is,
> Inter-assured of the mind,
> Care lesse, eyes, lips, and hands to misse.[3]

To Amoret, Vaughan addressed this idea with some revision:

> Just so base, Sublunarie Lovers hearts
> Fed on loose prophane desires,
>   May for an Eye,
>   Or face comply:
> But those removed, they will as soone depart,
>   And shew their Art,
>   And painted fires.

1. Martin, *The Works of Henry Vaughan*, i, 9.
2. *Ibid.*, p. 15.
3. Grierson, *Donne's Poetical Works*, i, 50.

Whil'st I by pow'rfull Love, so much refin'd,
That my absent soule the same is,
Carelesse to misse,
A glaunce, or kisse,
Can with those Elements of lust and sence,
Freely dispence,
And court the mind.[1]

Certainly *"the fire at highest is but* Platonick," and the revisions are instructive. Vaughan makes the idea didactic, dilutes it, and sacrifices some of its subtlety to music, thereby losing Donne's exciting concision. But this poem, in which the presence of Donne is clearly felt, has firmer structure than is general with Vaughan, against whom the charge is so often made that he lacked the sense of form, that he did not know when to stop. The poem ends with the conceit of the loadstones, which is a typical Radical image in the Donne manner, and which forms a structural climax for the thought.

Again, in *To Amoret gone from him,* where the Metaphysical influence is visibly felt, though the substance has the peculiar Vaughan flavor, the articulation of thought is tighter than usual. This check to the looseness which has helped us to regard Vaughan primarily as a poet of fine lines may be attributed, in my opinion, to the Metaphysical influence which here comes directly from Donne. In *The Lampe* a tighter structure is secured by the development of an extended conceit. This poem, which is very Don-

1. *Ibid.,* pp. 12–13.

nean in its sensuous thinking and homely images, begins with the fine lines,

> 'T is dead night round about: Horrour doth creepe
> And move on with the shades; stars nod, and sleepe,
> And through the dark aire spin a firie thread
> Such as doth gild the lazie glow-worms bed.[1]

Though faulty, *The Lampe* is one of the most perfect
poems in Vaughan, but it is a later poem and may
have been influenced by Herbert's use of the conceit.
None the less, it could have been written by no one
but Vaughan, though it inherits the mood of Donne
and the feeling peculiar to his sensibility.

The influence that made Vaughan a religious poet
came from Herbert and was later than the direct
Donne influence.[2] What he got from Herbert was
much more than the manner, — that he had already
got from Donne, — for the editors of both Herbert
and Vaughan are constantly noting Vaughan's borrowings from *The Temple* in figure, theme, and metre.
Much more than either Herbert or Crashaw, Vaughan
seems to have borrowed from the subject-matter of
other poets; especially has he leaned upon Herbert
in the titles and themes of his poems. Dependence to
the extent of his *Son-dayes* on the *Prayer* and *Sunday*
of Herbert is by no means unusual.[3] But the things
for which we prize Vaughan are drawn mostly from
himself, although they do not relinquish the Meta-

---

1. Martin, *The Works of Henry Vaughan*, ii, 410–411.
2. Martin's commentary shows how extensively Vaughan drew upon
Herbert.
3. See Martin's note to *Son-dayes*, *op. cit.*, ii, 698.

physical manner, which they could not very well do without.

One of the things for which we cherish him is that splendid image which introduces *The World*:

> I saw Eternity the other night
> Like a great *Ring* of pure and endless light
> All calm, as it was bright.

Although the last line may betray some secret influence — more than verbal — from Herbert's *Vertue*, the image is Vaughan's and a supreme example of the impassioned geometry of Donne, of the Radical image which is the friend of the mystic. Mr. Henry W. Wells says justly: "This type of image, as might readily be inferred, is a common resort of the mystic. Driven from the possibility of literal statement, he still confronts a mystery which demands some measure of expression." [1] But Donne had been before Vaughan "at the round earths imagin'd corners," and had pointed out the way. Vaughan himself has given us more than one happy example of how the conceit can snatch at success where expression fails the mystic. In *Quickness* he is trying to seize the essence of life; despairing, he ends thus:

> But life is, what none can express,
> *A quickness, which my God hath kist.*

In lines such as these we see one of the most powerful factors in Donne's influence on poets like Herbert, Crashaw, and Vaughan, and we understand why

---

1. *Poetic Imagery*, p. 131. Page 132 is also pertinent.

Carew and others felt that Donne had increased the possibilities of language. In such lines as this one from *The Night,*

> Gods silent, searching flight,

we feel the Vaughan who alone could have written them; and yet we feel as strongly that without Donne he might not have written them, or that if he had, they would not be the same. Not because he is mystical, but because he succeeded in thus capturing his mysticism in poetry do we prize him as a poet.

Since Vaughan, like Crashaw, missed the reasonable structure in Herbert and Donne, though perhaps less completely in his early poems, we need not be surprised that he is remembered for what appealed to him in other poets — lines and images. Perhaps the most sustained poem that Vaughan has left us, which at the same time keeps his peculiar essence, is the *Ascension-Hymn*; and yet our anthology version of this poem usually gives only the second part of the original under the title of *Friends Departed.*[1] The poem that many would choose, *The Retreate,* which owes much of its popularity to anticipations of certain things in Blake and Wordsworth, belongs to the Donne tradition because of its use of the conceit.

Though Vaughan's use of the conceit is simpler and less intellectual than Donne's and generally more impassioned than Crashaw's, it gives distinct character to his verse, and especially to those sacred

1. See Martin, *The Works of Henry Vaughan,* ii, 482, and *Oxford Book of English Verse,* p. 397.

poems we have chosen to remember, from *Regenera-tion* on. Perhaps no better example of this distinct character could be found than the *Ascension-Hymn*, which we remember chiefly by its wonderful line of mystical experience,

They are all gone into the world of light!

Scarcely less wonderful is the way Vaughan uses the conceit to illuminate this thought and to catch the very essence of his mysticism. Here we may surprise him at a characteristic moment:

If a star were confin'd into a Tomb
   Her captive flames must needs burn there;
But when the hand that lockt her up, gives room,
   She'l shine through all the sphaere.

Peculiar to Vaughan and beautiful as this is, it cannot be read thoughtfully without a reference to the Donne tradition, which makes it a product of its time as well as an expression of Vaughan himself.

In another way Vaughan is more like Crashaw than like Herbert or Donne: his feeling lacks the precision and outline that we find in theirs. Whether this loss comes from the fact that Vaughan misses much of the intellectual side of the Donne tradition, or from the fact that he is more mystical, it is a loss that can be definitely perceived, as well in the following comparison as anywhere. First, the passage from Herbert's *Whitsunday* that Vaughan imitates:

Listen, sweet Dove, unto my song
And spread thy golden wings in me;
Hatching my tender heart so long,
Till it get wing and flie away with thee.[1]

Now Vaughan's imitation in *Disorder and Frailty*:

O, is! but give wings to my fire,
And hatch my soul, untill it fly
Up where thou art, amongst thy tire
Of Stars, above Infirmity.[2]

The greater difficulty with which the images in the
Vaughan version are realized, the blurring of their
edges, deprives his feeling of the precision and outline
which define that of Herbert. This loss brings
Vaughan closer to Crashaw and distinguishes him
from Herbert and Donne, while it suggests the fate
that might have overtaken his feeling without the
discipline of the Metaphysical tradition. As a further
test for this distinction, one may compare the ways
in which Herbert and Vaughan realize the emotion of
peace in their poems on that subject.[3] In the flowing
music of Vaughan's poem one may detect the very
tone of Wordsworth's "old, unhappy, far-off things"
— a strange contrast to the clarity and definiteness
of Herbert.

As a poet of Nature Vaughan is partial to evening
and night, to twilight regions where Nature speaks
to him in pantheistic terms that anticipate Words-

1. Palmer, *op. cit.*, ii, 157.
2. Martin, *The Works of Henry Vaughan*, ii, 446.
3. Palmer, *op. cit.*, ii, 377; and Martin, *ibid.*, p. 430.

worth, and where he may become reminiscent of childhood. But in *The Charnel-house* he echoes the mood of Donne, catching the very manner of thought of the *Second Anniversarie* in lines like

> Think then, that in this bed
> There sleep the Reliques of as proud a head
> As stern and subtill as your own.[1]

These two dimensions of his thought, together with the third of his mysticism, make it possible to regard him as more nineteenth-century than any of his contemporaries; but the Donne dimension requires that we insist on his being a true child of his age. And in my opinion we must conclude that, in spite of the naturally simple style of Vaughan, he is the poet of supreme lines and images that we know largely because he felt the power of the Donne tradition, though most strongly in the disciple, George Herbert.

1. *Ibid.*, i, 42. This is an early poem.

VI. THE PROFANE LINE

THE profane line of Metaphysical poetry cannot be properly distinguished from the sacred line, except in a certain predominance of worldly subject-matter. While the poets in the profane line often write religious verse, their natural talent is more congenial to secular subjects, and their finest achievements belong to the poetry of love. By some quirk of fate the Herbert family gave us the first representative on each side of the Donne tradition. Indeed, there is something like poetic justice in the fact that to Lady Magdalen Herbert, who earned the grateful regard of Donne, must go the credit of giving the two poet sons who established his tradition. Thereafter, the profane line carried on the mode of making love with the brain as well as with the heart.

LORD HERBERT OF CHERBURY

Lord Herbert, probably the earliest of Donne's imitators, received the somewhat ironical compliment of imitation from Donne. Drummond quotes Jonson as saying "That Done said to him, he wrott that Epitaph on Prince Henry *Look to me, Faith* to match Sir Ed: Herbert in obscurenesse." The poem that Donne sought to match was Lord Herbert's *Elegy for the Prince*. Both of these poems develop elaborate

conceits in the manner in which Donne set the fashion. Since the *Elegy* exhibits the worst side of this
fashion, Donne was paying himself a rather doubtful
compliment when he matched Lord Herbert. The
most interesting item in this statement is the quality
marked out for imitation, especially if we connect it
with Chapman's words on obscurity and reflect that
obscureness was probably regarded as fashionable,
was indeed part of the doctrine of keeping knowledge
from the vulgar.

While Lord Herbert's *Elegy* reflects the unhappy
side of the Donne tradition, his best poems reflect the
happy side and miss the defects of the Metaphysical
qualities. It is not without significance that this
poet, who was first a philosopher, should take to the
manner of Donne. We could scarcely ask for a better example of the assertion of the philosophic side of
the conflict between philosophy and poetry which
disturbed the Elizabethan mind. Vain as Lord Herbert was, his poetry does not seem to have been part
of his vanity; so we may infer that it was affinity, and
not fashion, that drew him to the Metaphysical
method. But Lord Herbert's discipleship is much
more certain than his poetic worth, if we are to judge
by the number of the happy few who have praised
him. Mr. Churton Collins, Sir Sidney Lee, Swinburne, and Mr. Moore Smith compose almost the
whole catalogue of those who have spoken in his
favor. For the Donne tradition he is important because he contributed a few lovely poems and because
he was the first to imitate the love songs of Donne,

just as his brother was the first to imitate the divine poems.

Mr. Churton Collins, the first editor of Lord Herbert's poems since the original edition of 1665,[1] noted the Metaphysical character of Lord Herbert in his edition of 1881. What distinguishes Lord Herbert's love poetry from the Courtly sort is the way of thinking and feeling represented by the Metaphysical conceit. Despite other likenesses, it is this that makes his verses, like those of King and Marvell, belong to the Donne tradition and not to the Jonson tradition. Chiefly, one feels, it is a kind of intellectual toughness that keeps this poetry from the prettiness of the Cavalier lyric or the neatness of the Jonson song. Much as I admire these things in Herrick or Carew, I would not willingly dispense with the less easy importunities of the Metaphysical love poets. As it will be remembered, Dryden regretted Donne's love poems for similar reasons, and like a blushing girl, preferred what we call the language of the heart. But let us see what the real effect of the Donne influence was upon the songs of an accomplished courtier.

An Ode upon a Question moved, Whether Love should continue for ever? brings us straight upon the language Corinna heard from Lord Herbert of Cherbury. In it we discover the impassioned geometry, the mixture of philosophy and emotion, the chain of reasoning, and the conceit which we found

1. As with Donne, his poems were not published till after his death in 1648, but they were known by the poets.

in Donne. The Platonism of this *Ode* is of the sort
we find in Donne's *Extasie*: while it argues the union
of souls, it does not scorn the body and the use of
sense. At the same time this *Ode* reveals the rational
evolution so common in Donne and not infrequent in
Lord Herbert, though it lacks the full-blooded realism
of Donne and something of his sensuous perception
of thought. Its music is its own, and interesting
because it derives from Lord Herbert's longest and
finest use of the *In Memoriam* metre. If we would
hear this music murmuring in the impassioned geometry and conceit of Donne, we have only to turn to
such a stanza as

> That if affection be a line,
>> Which is clos'd up in our last hour;
>> Oh how 't would grieve me, any pow'r
> Could force so dear a love as mine!

This is the sort of love poetry we owe to the Donne
tradition. The method of this Metaphysical poetry
goes back to Dante, whence Donne may have drawn
it, since we know that he read Dante, and since the
resemblances between the two, different as they may
be, are often too compelling to be disregarded. For
poets in this tradition, love strikes fire in the intellect and philosophy itself becomes the language of
adoration. Whether Corinna should hear such things,
only became a problem with a later generation.

The most beautiful passage in Lord Herbert's *Ode*
pays the same kind of adoration to Corinna and
renders even greater homage to Donne:

So when from hence we shall be gone,
   And be no more, nor you, nor I,
   As one anothers mystery,
Each shall be both, yet both but one.

This said, in her up-lifted face,
   Her eyes which did that beauty crown,
   Were like two starrs, that having faln down,
Look up again to find their place:

While such a moveless silent peace
   Did seize on their becalmed sense,
   One would have thought some Influence
Their ravish'd spirits did possess.

The lovely simile of the stars is thoughtful and not instantly grasped, but justified because it interprets feeling in a new and subtle way. The word *becalmed* acquires and gives an extraordinary richness of association, while *influence* connects the stars with spirits, and gives an aura to the riot of the senses that reminds us of the *Extasie*. Although the *Ode* has its Platonism, it is Platonism as touched by Donne and not by Spenser. In such love poetry we are far from the *Amoretti* and yet, however nearer, not one with *Lucasta*, for this is the way of thinking and feeling that we find in Donne.

The significant vehicle of this mode of thought and feeling is the conceit as it appears in the lines,

When again all these rare perfections meet,
Composed in the circle of thy face,[1]

1. *To a Lady who did sing excellently*, Moore Smith, *The Poems of Lord Herbert of Cherbury*, p. 44.

where the feeling is condensed in a circle of subtle thought. Or we may turn to one of the finest poems Lord Herbert ever wrote and find the same vehicle expressing the same kind of thinking and feeling. Read again the first stanza of the *Elegy over a Tomb*:

> Must I then see, alas! eternal night
>   Sitting upon those fairest eyes,
> And closing all those beams, which once did rise
>   So radiant and bright,
> That light and heat in them to us did prove
>   Knowledge and Love?

Here we are close to the secret of Metaphysical expression, to the intellectual excitement that emotion produced in these poets and that in turn created the expression of this emotion. Their feeling for a girl did generate both light and heat, and did prove knowledge and love; and in these qualities Lord Herbert's stanza is characteristic of Metaphysical love poetry. The rest of his *Elegy* develops an extended comparison, which is one form the conceit took in this poetry.

This characteristic intellectual excitement may be illustrated in another poem of his which admirably reveals the peculiar Metaphysical combination of rational processes, colloquial directness, and passionate feeling. The poem in question is the continuation of *To her Mind* which Mr. Moore Smith entitles *Loves End*. One cannot read this poem without recalling the very accent of Donne's voice in *The Dreame* or without looking forward to Browning:

Thus ends my Love, but this doth grieve me most,
   That so it ends, but that ends too, this yet,
Besides the Wishes, hopes and time I lost,
   Troubles my mind awhile, that I am set
Free, worse then deny'd: I can neither boast
   Choice nor success, as my Case is, nor get
Pardon from my self, that I loved not
   A better Mistress, or her worse; this Debt
Only's her due, still, that she be forgot
Ere chang'd, lest I love none; this done, the taint
   Of foul Inconstancy is clear'd at least
In me, there only rests but to unpaint
   Her form in my mind, that so dispossest
It be a Temple, but without a Saint.

The rapid alterations and antitheses of thought and feeling, with the consequent elliptical expression, cannot be mistaken; they could come from no poet ignorant of Donne; in fact, they will not be heard again with the same genuine accent till we come to Browning. Even an emotion so strong and so far from reason as betrayed love set these Metaphysical poets furiously to think. The converse of this is that learning set these poets ardently to feel. It is perhaps not irrelevant to recall the effect which love had on the mind, and ideas on the emotions, of a Lucretius; the difference is chiefly one of philosophical compass, not one of kind.

I have dwelt on the influence of Donne on the lyric poetry of Lord Herbert because his editors have been readier to admit such an influence on his poems in heroic measures. Furthermore, Lord Herbert uses phrases from Donne in *A Description* and echoes his charnel-house mood in *To his Mistress*, while his verses to *The Green-Sickness Beauty* and to *The Brown Beauty* were probably inspired by Donne. Along with such superficial influences go many deeper ones, of which the argumentative development in *The Idea* is an example, or the woven texture of his *Elegy for Doctor* Dunn. Perhaps the most flattering critical testimony to the closeness with which Lord Herbert followed Donne is the fact that the doubtful poem, *Ode: Of our Sense of Sinne*, finds a place both in Grierson's edition of Donne and in Moore Smith's edition of Lord Herbert. Likewise, both poets share the critical censure for obscurity and rough verse.

But Lord Herbert's music is his own. Occasionally he uses one of Donne's favorite measures, as in *The Idea*; but usually he experiments for himself. The harmony which he gets from the *In Memoriam* metre — first used by Jonson — is fully up to that of Tennyson, and it is this harmony that gives his *Ode* a measure of superiority over the *Elegy over a Tomb*. In contrast, there is the harshness of his heroic measures, which we no sooner remember than we forget in the haunting music of "*Tears, flow no more*," or "*If you refuse me once*." The music in such lyrics as these comes closer to the massive harmony of Donne than to the charming tinkle of much Cavalier verse, while the texture is far richer in Metaphysical suggestion, in what has been called "metaphysical stimulants." Into this music, as in Donne, division frequently creeps, often to give us the happiest harmony.

If the last couplet in *To his Mistress* shows how the Donne influence could bring out the worst in Lord Herbert, such lovely poems as the *Elegy over a Tomb* and *An Ode upon a Question moved* are enough to show that the same influence could bring out the finest. The master of whom Lord Herbert wrote

> Let therefore none
> Hope to find out an Idiom and sense,
> Equal to thee, and to thy Eminence,[1]

thus continued his intellectual tradition in the poetry of Lord Herbert, who was probably the first to imitate his love songs and so to establish a tradition of love poetry whose last great exemplar was Robert Browning. The wisdom of Lady Magdalen Herbert in recognizing the genius of Donne was not lost on her two poet sons, to whom English poetry is not a little indebted.

HENRY KING

Henry King, Bishop of Chichester, has met a fate similar to that of Lord Herbert. He is remembered for a few poems; and one, *The Exequy*, is among the finest of the century, along with Lord Herbert's *Ode*. Bishop King was a closer friend of Donne than Lord Herbert, for he served as literary executor of the great Dean of St. Paul's. Like many of the seventeenth-century poets, King wrote an elegy for the death of Donne. In this elegy he repeats many of the praises we found in Carew's elegy; but such repeti-

1. *Elegy for Doctor* Dunn, Moore Smith, *op. cit.*, p. 57.

tion is not unusual, for most of the elegists of Donne echo the praises of Carew, thereby indicating a consensus of opinion, and perhaps some imitation. What is unusual in King's elegy is that he does not try quite so hard as the other poets to imitate the style of Donne while praising him. Particularly in contrast to Lord Herbert, he is so much less obscure and so much closer to the Waller couplet that we wonder at his discipleship to Donne.

But in other ways King is much closer to Donne than Lord Herbert is. Though so much less obscure, King makes far greater use of the homely word and the figure drawn from the near-at-hand that we find in Donne. But King also makes frequent use of the learned image, as a poem like *The Legacy* will show, recalling the practice of Donne and even the legal figures of Shakspere. Let me quote a stanza from this same poem to show how near King often came to Donne's way of thinking and feeling:

> With this cast ragge of my mortalitie
> Let all my faults and errours buried be.
> And as my sear-cloth rots, so may kind fate
> Those worse acts of my life incinerate.
>   He shall in story fill a glorious room
>   Whose ashes and whose sins sleep in one Tomb.

Witness the homely conceit in the "cast ragge of my mortalitie," the learned word *incinerate*, and the presence of one of Donne's favorite figures in "a glorious room." Though the verse suggests the orientation toward Waller, the emotion and its manner of realization are those of Donne, and are by no means to be

confused with those of the beautiful Cavalier lyric
"*Tell me no more how fair she is,*" in which the neatness of Jonson inspires the verse.

In King's elegy to Donne we find that he salutes
two things in Donne: the "summes of wit" that he
lent to his age, and

> that awful fire, which once did burn
> In thy clear brain, now fall'n into thy Urn.

It is the absence of these distinctive qualities that
keeps the lovely "*Tell me no more*" from any real
place in the Donne tradition, just as it is the presence
of such qualities in *The Surrender* or *The Exequy* that
makes them a part of the same tradition. King
spends these sums of wit most freely in his elegies,
but only when he is deeply moved does his verse
catch something of the awful intensity of Donne,
though flashes of it are not infrequent. In *An Acknowledgment*, where there are plentiful sums of this
wit, we encounter this passage:

> But the black Map of death and discontent
> Behind that Adamantine firmament,
> That luckless figure which like Calvary
> Stands strew'd and coppy'd out in skuls, is I:
> Whose life your absence clouds, and makes my time
> Move blindfold in the dark ecliptick line.

Throughout this verse, and especially in the splendid
conceit of the last couplet, we feel the presence of
that awful fire which King praised in Donne, and
sometimes captured.

Even in the *Sonnets* of King the intrusion of
Donne's manner seems to bring a firmer and a richer
texture to the verse. Charming as "*Tell me no more*"
is, it is a little thin by the side of this stanza from
another *Sonnet*:

> Dry those fair, those chrystal eyes
> Which like growing fountains rise
> To drown their banks. Griefs sullen brooks
> Would better flow in furrow'd looks.
>   Thy lovely face was never meant
>   To be the shoar of discontent.

Here the Metaphysical method enriches the associa-
tions and thus adds to the texture of the emotional
expression, producing a new density of feeling. The
intrusion of Donne into the *Sonnets* of King is reflected to the extent of colloquial and even homely
words, condensed and extended conceits, the startling opening, and something of the rational progression. *The Surrender* and *The Legacy* have similar
qualities, some in greater degree, though marked by
the grave and tender feeling of King.

Since Tennyson seems to have matched his *Love
and Duty* against King's *Surrender*, or at least to have
encouraged such matching by his readers, we may
compare them as products of their centuries. In
King's poem one feels that his emotion has been
much more definitely placed in a structure of human
emotions, and that it is the truer for that orientation
and subtle recognition of other points of view. Then
King's feeling is much more astringently expressed.
In Tennyson's poem the emotion is a trifle hysterical

and at the same time lost, like the thought, in a mass
of decorative verbiage; while the poem itself reveals
a tendency to think and feel by starts, which compares unfavorably with King's poem. In such a comparison the palm must go to the seventeenth century,
which possessed something that often made a lesser
poet superior to a nineteenth-century poet in his expression of the same feeling. This something is to be
found in the sensibility of Donne, which gave the
Metaphysical poets a method of coping with experience that a poet like Catullus derived from a
whole civilization. Briefly, one may describe it as a
working habit of mind, or as the ability to use all
kinds of experience with a just sense of their human
values; concretely, one may illustrate it in Donne's
sense of the interdependence of mind and body.
Donne was capable of unifying not only the passion
and levity of Catullus, but also the thought of Lucretius and the divinity of Andrewes.

This method, in so far as he could use it, was part
of King's Metaphysical inheritance. Let us see what
it did for his finest poem, *The Exequy*. The metre of
this poem is the same as that of Crashaw's *Saint
Teresa* and Marvell's *Coy Mistress*; and again it
yields a new music, making one wonder at the variety
of which it is capable. The emotion of this poem is
rendered with a precision that makes the feeling in a
poem like Tennyson's *Love and Duty* seem vague and
incompletely realized. Closer inspection shows how
this precision is achieved by the bright clear out-
lines of the conceits, whose clearness enhances their

emotional auras and makes them as poignant as simplicity. This quality appears when King, expressing his grief at the death of his wife, exclaims between his tears,

> thou art the book,
> The library whereon I look
> Though almost blind.

Or again we catch this precise and powerful suggestiveness in the astronomical figure which is pointed in these lines:

> And twixt me and my soules dear wish
> The earth now interposed is,
> Which such a strange eclipse doth make
> As ne're was read in Almanake.

Notice the extraordinary richness of association that *earth* receives and lends in this context. It is surely one of the triumphs of the conceit that it can give to the earth which separates a man from his dead wife the plangent suggestions that here enrich the imagination. When a little farther on in the poem King remembers how the earth must end before he can see his loved one again, we find the conceit thrusting a learned word into a position of great suggestiveness:

> And a fierce Feaver must calcine
> The body of this world like thine.

Calcine is not what we call a poetic word, but look at the powerful metaphorical relation that it brings to this emotion!

Among the conceits of this poem there are several extended comparisons, but none finer than the one in which King represents his anxiety to see his dead wife, under the figure of a journey. This figure, like the others, lends structural outline to the thought which it develops:

> Stay for me there; I will not faile
> To meet thee in that hollow Vale.
> And think not much of my delay;
> I am already on the way,
> And follow thee with all the speed
> Desire can make, or sorrows breed.
> Each minute is a short degree,
> And ev'ry houre a step towards thee.
> At night when I betake to rest,
> Next morn I rise neerer my West
> Of life, almost by eight houres saile,
> Then when sleep breath'd his drowsie gale . . .
> But heark! My pulse like a soft Drum
> Beats my approach, tells *Thee* I come;
> And slow howere my marches be,
> I shall at last sit down by *Thee*.

By means of the figure in the last lines, King invests the simple functioning of the body with an effect of terror that intensifies the emotion he is expressing. In *My Midnight Meditation* he has used the same figure to illustrate the ancient feeling of the fugitiveness of life:

> The beating of thy pulse (when thou art well)
> Is just the tolling of thy Passing Bell.

This conceit, with the substitution of bell for drum,

is less effective; but either is a happy addition to the
list of commonplaces by which poets have expressed
this feeling, and either is invested with a terror that
is rarely achieved.

While *The Exequy* is suffused with the grave and
tender feeling of King, it owes much of its peculiar
magic to the Metaphysical tradition. If the reader
will now turn to Tennyson's *Love and Duty*, he will
understand what I mean when I say that there was
something in the seventeenth-century temper that
made a poem on the same feeling, like King's *Surrender*, superior in expression to that of Tennyson.
On the other hand, such a poem as *The Labyrinth*,
though strongly marked by the Metaphysical tradition, shows how the couplet of King is moving in the
direction of Pope. Many of the couplets of this poem
have the polished antithetical form of Pope. But it is
not in such things that the merit of King lies; rather
it is in the qualities which I have illustrated in his
Metaphysical verse. Even *A Contemplation upon
Flowers*, though it may not be his, owes something to
the influence that made *The Exequy* so distinctive a
product of its time and so fine a tribute to the Donne
tradition.

Like many poets of that time whose work rises
superior to mere fashion, King found the Donne way
of thinking and feeling congenial to the expression
of his native talent. For such poets, Donne was not
a fashion: he was a monarch of wit who taught them
in poetry that

So Jewellers no Art or Metal trust
To form the Diamond, but the Diamonds dust.[1]

Unfortunately, both Donne and his followers, but especially his followers, were at times deceived by paste gems. Among such gems, however, we cannot number poems like *The Surrender* and *The Exequy*.

ANDREW MARVELL

Andrew Marvell is remembered as the author of the finest Horatian ode in the English language. He is less known, but no less deserving, as the finest Metaphysical poet after Donne, whom he surpasses at times. Regarded in the light of his poetry, the fact that he was a Puritan is a tribute to the persuasion of his Latin culture and to the urgency of his Metaphysical sensibility. The power of these literary inheritances preserved his poetry from the fate which overtook Milton's when he renounced sensuousness: they made Marvell more a poet of his age than a Puritan. Yet these two influences were really one, for Donne had combined the sensuous strain and urbane wit of the Latin poets with the dialectics of medieval love poetry when he fathered the Metaphysical tradition. But Marvell, like Jonson, caught more of the art of these classical poets.

In the sensuousness of his poetry Marvell reminds us of a more rational, unmystical Crashaw. He has

---

1. King's elegy on Donne. My quotations from King rely on the text of Dr. Lawrence Mason, except for *The Exequy*, which is in Grierson's version. Professor Saintsbury gives a modernized text in *Caroline Poets*, vol. iii.

the same sensuous apprehension of thought that is so
marked in the Metaphysicals and that is censured
by Courthope when he objects to the materialism of
the images by which Herbert represents the Holy
Communion as a "Banquet." [1] Precisely the same
quality of thought is to be found in such a poem as
Marvell's *Nymph and the Fawn,* and is the source of
its strength. The Metaphysical combination of ratiocinative processes, colloquial directness, and passionate feeling finds a superb medium in this faculty
for concrete expression which the conceit embodied.

Though a Puritan, Marvell did not repudiate this
sensuousness as Milton eventually did, but accepted
it as an element native to his Latin and Metaphysical
inheritance. Being a man of less independent mind,
Marvell became more a product of tradition and an
expression of his literary age than did Milton. There
are times when Marvell's poems seem distilled from
the very air about him. This does not mean that he
has not a distinctive talent of his own, or that his
mind is less interesting than Milton's; but it does
mean that his verse makes us conscious of the penetrating influence of a literary inheritance. Compared
with a poet like Milton, who created his own literary
medium, Marvell is a supreme example of the poet
who discovers his talent in the current of a literary
tradition.

Marvell's poetry unites all the Metaphysical
qualities with a more abiding sense of art than the
other Metaphysicals display. In him the influence

1. See Courthope, *History of English Poetry,* iii, 218.

of Latin poets like Horace seems to have moderated many, though not all, of the extravagant tendencies of the Metaphysical tradition; but it has tempered them without dimming their essential virtues. For instance, the rational evolution of Donne's songs may be found admirably employed in poems like *The Definition of Love*, *To his Coy Mistress*, or *Clorinda and Damon*, but employed with less rigor and more reticence. The homely and learned images, the wit, passionate feeling, and massive music of Donne likewise appear, and are likewise moderated. But the lighter side of Donne's wit, his levity, is stronger in Marvell than in any Metaphysical we have so far considered, though the Cavalier poets have it in plenty. Most of Donne's close followers were rather solemn men, except Lord Herbert and Crashaw, who were not devoid of levity or the spark of urbane wit. However, wit is the quality which Donne shares most liberally with his age.

As in the other Metaphysical poets, the conceit in Marvell is significant as representing a particular way of thinking and feeling. The so much admired conclusion to *An Epitaph* suggests why the Waller manner was inadequate for the expression of Marvell's thought and feeling:

> Modest as Morn; as Mid-day bright;
> Gentle as Ev'ning; cool as Night;
> 'T is true: but all so weakly said;
> 'T were more Significant, *She's dead*.

True, but all too weakly said to express the sort of emotion which stirred in Marvell when he wrote the

Coy Mistress or *Bermudas*; even here, better say with Donne, "Shee, shee is dead; shee's dead." But most significant of all is the use of the conceit to establish connections with plangent waves of emotion and subtle nebulas of thought. Here are examples of such employment:

C. Near this, a Fountaines liquid Bell
Tinkles within the concave Shell.

D. Might a Soul bath there and be clean,
Or slake its Drought?[1]

So weeps the wounded Balsome: so
The holy Frankincense doth flow.
The brotherless *Heliades*
Melt in such Amber Tears as these.[2]

O then let me in time compound,
And parly with those conquering Eyes;
Ere they have try'd their force to wound,
Ere, with their glancing wheels, they drive
In Triumph over Hearts that strive,
And them that yield but more despise.[3]

In these passages the poet forces upon relatively simple things the connection which reveals a hidden prospect of terror and wonder in the affairs of common life. A continual source of amazement is the iron that is discovered in the soul of this porcelain-like poetry, whose singular artificiality contains the strangest vistas of emotion. The conceits in these

1. Margoliouth, *Marvell's Poems & Letters*, i, 18.
2. *The Nymph and the Fawn, ibid.*, p. 24.
3. *The Picture of little T. C., ibid.*, p. 38.

passages are structural decorations which support
the emotions of the poetry.

In *The Definition of Love* the more toughly intellectual conceit receives characteristic employment
and represents the impassioned geometry of Donne:

> As Lines so Loves *oblique* may well
> Themselves in every Angle greet:
> But ours so truly *Paralel*,
> Though infinite can never meet.

Although this poem is made of such conceits as this,
the more extended conceit also appears, but less obviously than in such a poem as *The Gallery*. While
Marvell's sense of art is surer than that of any of the
other Metaphysicals, his conceits sometimes fail to be
as serious or as effective as he intended. In this respect
his *Eyes and Tears* is a tissue of success and failure,
ranging from failures like

> These Tears which better measure all,
> Like wat'ry Lines and Plummets fall,[1]

to successes like

> And Stars shew lovely in the Night,
> But as they seem the Tears of Light.[2]

Likewise, *Upon Appleton House* has a fairly large
number of figures which miscarry, but Marvell's truly
memorable poems do not slip into such faults while
the conceit etches their feeling upon our imagination.

Marvell gave supreme form to the Metaphysical
qualities in his *Coy Mistress*, which, compared with

1. Margoliouth, *op. cit.*, i, 15.   2. *Ibid.*, p. 16.

Waller's "*Go, lovely Rose,*" reveals the Metaphysical ability to give power and perspective to emotion. Both poems urge the admonition of the Ausonian rose; but Marvell's poem captures more of a Latin grandeur and reverberation, is articulated by a tough reasonableness, is supported by conceits commanding profound vistas, and is expressed with a kind of bronze music, urbane wit, and soaring passion. Beginning with a play of urbane wit, Marvell addresses his coy mistress,

> Had we but World enough, and Time,
> This coyness Lady were no crime,

and then after indulging this fancy he suddenly turns, with a profound sweep of passion and imagery and imaginative surprise, to the metaphysical reality underlying this play of wit,

> But at my back I alwaies hear
> Times winged Charriot hurrying near:
> And yonder all before us lye
> Desarts of vast Eternity . . .
> The Grave's a fine and private place,
> But none I think do there embrace.

Having inextricably mingled levity and seriousness in the last couplet, Marvell concludes,

> Let us roll all our Strength, and all
> Our sweetness, up into one Ball:
> And tear our Pleasures with rough strife,
> Thorough the Iron gates of Life.

The effect of weight and comprehensiveness which the conceit gives Marvell's theme cannot be matched

in Waller's *"Go, lovely Rose"* which has the Restoration prettiness but none of the Metaphysical
strength that distinguishes poems like King's *Exequy*
or Lord Herbert's *Ode*. In spite of the seeming artificiality and trivial character of many of Marvell's
themes, his poems acquire an effect of seriousness and
solidity from his use of the Metaphysical method.

The note of artificiality in Marvell is related to his
way of seeing Nature, before which his imagination
never "vainly flapt its Tinsel Wing." Since Marvell
is so often regarded as a poet who, like Vaughan,
shows an almost nineteenth-century gift for observ-
ing Nature, it is necessary to call attention to the
truly seventeenth-century character of this gift. Despite the intimacy of Marvell's feeling for Nature,
his *Garden* is closer to the Nature of Milton's early
poems, to the Nature of *Comus* and *Lycidas*, than it is
to that of any nineteenth-century poet. For once
that he says,

> My Soul into the boughs does glide,[1]

there are a dozen occasions when Nature appears to
him in this fashion:

> For now the Waves are fal'n and dry'd,
> And now the Meadows fresher dy'd;
> Whose Grass, with moister colour dasht,
> Seems as green Silks but newly washt.[2]

Professor Margoliouth tells us that *green* is one
of Marvell's favorite epithets, occurring twenty-five

1. *The Garden*, Margoliouth, *op. cit.*, i, 49, stanza vii.
2. *Upon Appleton House*, *ibid.*, p. 78, stanza lxxix.

times in the 1681 volume.[1] This fact is indicative of
the way in which Marvell worked Nature into the
tapestry of his verse.

Both his artifice and his parterre of Nature succeed
in communicating genuine emotion, and that is their
mystery. As strong a sense of artifice as can be
found in Marvell appears in *The Nymph and the
Fawn*, and yet the emotion is unusually moving for
so slight a subject. Compelled to account for this
artifice, we are likely to find most of it in the images,
which have a concreteness that makes tears like a
gum and lends the durable outline of paper petals to
real flowers. Just as in the thought of the nymph
herself, the feeling of the poem becomes a garden
group cut in marble and placed in a Nature that resembles a lawn party lit by Japanese lanterns. In
fact, the emotions are engraved by the conceits in
much the same fashion that Nature is represented by
the *décor* of artificial gardens, as in Japanese painting
and yet with the suggestiveness of true poetry,

> Annihilating all that's made
> To a green Thought in a green Shade.[2]

While *Upon Appleton House* has moments when
Nature is seen with more directness, it never loses
sight of the Nature that

> hangs in shades the Orange bright,
> Like golden Lamps in a green Night.[3]

1. See Margoliouth, *op. cit.*, i, 219, note to l. 23.
2. *The Garden, ibid.*, p. 49.
3. *Bermudas, ibid.*, p. 17.

This porcelain artifice I take to be Marvell's most
individual quality and a trait which, given the conceit, is capable of producing the most extraordinary
emotional connections for slight themes, or the most
enamel-like finish for iron thoughts. How different
are the effects which the conceit drew out of Nature
for two such poets as Marvell and Vaughan! For
Marvell one feels that Nature wears an attire more
like that which it wears for Mallarmé.

The artifice that permitted Marvell to see grass as
"green Silks" reflects a certain susceptibility to the
French spirit of the age, while the mixture of Biblical
and exotic images is an index to the interests of Marvell and to the complexity of his emotions. To be
sure, it was the wit of Donne that first achieved this
combination of levity and seriousness, touched with
the fantastic; the wit of Jonson had the same intellectual basis, but it was not characterized by "green
thoughts." The typical levity of Marvell may be
found in the images of the first paragraph of his *Coy
Mistress*, and it will be found reminiscent of Donne
rather than of Jonson.

Let us look at some of the images in this paragraph.

> I would
> Love you ten years before the Flood:
> And you should if you please refuse
> Till the Conversion of the *Jews*.
> My vegetable Love should grow
> Vaster than Empires, and more slow.

Such witty images as "my vegetable Love" and "till
the Conversion of the Jews" carry us back to the sort

we find in Donne's *Flea* or "*Go and catch a falling star.*" They have that touch of the fantastic which recalls the wit of Donne and divorces them, if ever so slightly, from the wit of Ben Jonson, which appears in these lines:

> Cannot we delude the eyes
> Of a few poor household spies;
> Or his easier ears beguile,
> So removed by our wile?
> 'T is no sin love's fruit to steal,
> But the sweet theft to reveal:
> To be taken, to be seen,
> These have crimes accounted been.[1]

As T. S. Eliot has said, there is a similar alliance of levity and seriousness, and an intensification of the seriousness by the levity, in these lines from Marvell and Jonson.[2] But this similarity, however important to an analysis of wit in seventeenth-century poetry, should not blind us to the difference which sets Marvell's wit apart from Jonson's and makes it of the same sort as Donne's. Even in the *Horatian Ode* Marvell's wit does not escape this touch of the fantastic, persuasive as his Latin culture is in that poem:

> The *Pict* no shelter now shall find
> Within his party-coloured Mind;
> But from this Valour sad
> Shrink underneath the Plad.[3]

With such examples before me, I do not think that I

---

1. *The Forest*, no. v, ed. Gifford-Cunningham, iii, 266.
2. *Homage to John Dryden*, p. 38.
3. Margoliouth, *op. cit.*, i, 90.

am forcing the relation of this quality to Donne; nor do I feel that either Jonson or Latin culture is sufficient to explain the presence of this intellectual and sophisticated wit in Marvell. However, it must be said that this *Ode* reveals the Marvell who, of the profane Metaphysicals, was the most perfect in music and diction, and also the most European.

Before we condemn the artificial in Marvell we should remember that Milton is the supreme master of an artificial style beside which Marvell's brocade of images is venial indeed. Before we dismiss the influence of Donne on Marvell we should read Marvell's *First Anniversary*, whose attribution to Waller in the *State Poems* of 1707 is an irony that Dryden should have lived to see. Aside from the difference of individual talent, what separates Marvell and Milton, who were so close in politics and religion, is nothing less than the Donne tradition, which gave Marvell the means of absorbing all kinds of experience and of fusing the most diverse.

And chief of such means was the wit which is so apt at rendering the complicated feelings of civilized society. This wit paid deference to the notion that one feeling shall not be allowed to reveal itself naked at the expense of another, that the dogmatism of a single feeling is not urbane; and to the notion that one feeling or experience must be able to endure the scrutiny of another, as genuine seriousness endures the scrutiny of real levity and real levity intensifies genuine seriousness. It was similar wit that enabled Catullus to reveal more of the whole man to his

Lesbia than we can find revealed in the better self which Browning turned to Elizabeth Barrett.

This wit was part and parcel of the Donne sensibility, which enabled his poetry to achieve an internal equilibrium that could include all sorts of experience and need repudiate none. From this sensibility Marvell and the other Metaphysicals reaped the benefits which I have tried to analyze in their poetry. Intense as Donne is, and whatever may be said of his followers, one can scarcely say that their emotions protest too much, or at the expense of the other human faculties.

AURELIAN TOWNSHEND

Aurelian Townshend rightly belongs among the minor Metaphysical poets, but of them he is probably the most interesting and the most individual. Therefore, I have chosen to include him among the major poets of this tradition so that I might illustrate the lesser poets who felt the influence of Donne. With him one could place such poets as Kynaston, Godolphin, and John Hall, but one would not thereby change appreciably the portrait of a minor Metaphysical poet. Of the four, Townshend seems to have the most individual talent, and Godolphin to be the least Metaphysical.

But all of them could write that soaring Caroline lyric to which Donne lent the strange witchcraft of Metaphysical suggestion, and perhaps the peculiar *élan*. Hear Kynaston to Cynthia *On concealment of her beauty*:

Do not conceale thy radiant eyes,
The starre-light of serenest skies,
Least wanting of their heavenly light,
They turne to *Chaos* endlesse night.

Or catch Godolphin in one of his finest moments of song:

Noe more unto my thoughts appeare,
Att least appeare lesse fayre,
For crazy tempers justly feare
The goodnesse of the ayre.[1]

And then listen to John Hall in his song to Romira, *The Call*:

See see the Sunne
Does slowly to his azure Lodging run,
Come sit but here
And presently hee'l quit our Hemisphere,
So still among
Lovers, time is too short or else too long;
Here will we spin
Legends for them that have Love Martyrs been,
Here on this plain
Wee'l talk Narcissus to a flour again.

While these fragments may not sufficiently reveal the Metaphysical quality of these songs, they cannot fail to suggest the wonderful marriage of rhythm and thought which belongs to the magic of the Caroline lyric. But to appreciate the charm of the minor Metaphysical lyric, we have only to analyze the talent of the poet with whom we began.

The "faint, pleasing tinkle of Aurelian Townshend" is the individual tone which he brought to the

1. *Song*, Grierson, *Metaphysical Poetry*, p. 45.

Metaphysical song. In his pastoral verse it is the tinkle of the lamb's bell, and may be heard in such a line as

> And noe lambe bleat, to breake thy sleepe.

Sometimes it is deepened or mellowed by a note of passion, and sometimes it merits the implication of Carew's question,

> Why dost thou sound, my dear Aurelian,
> In so shrill accents from thy Barbican?

But Townshend's slight music is capable of dainty argumentative passion and some of the strange reaches of the Metaphysical conceit, no less than of the pastoral charm of Marvell.

These qualities of Townshend may best be shown in a piece which Professor Grierson does not quote in his *Metaphysical Poetry*, the charming *Dialogue betwixt Time and a Pilgrime.*[1]

> *Pilgr.* Aged man, that mowes these fields.
> *Time.* Pilgrime speak, what is thy will?
> *Pilgr.* Whose soile is this that such sweet Pasture yields?
> Or who art thou whose Foot stand never still?
> Or where am I? *Time.* In love.
> *Pilgr.* His Lordship lies above.
> *Time.* Yes and below, and round about
> Where in all sorts of flow'rs are growing
> Which as the early Spring puts out,
> Time fals as fast a mowing.
> *Pilgr.* If thou art Time, these Flow'rs have Lives,
> And then I fear,
> Under some Lilly she I love
> May now be growing there.

---

1. For other pastoral poems see the E. K. Chambers edition.

Time. And in some Thistle or some spyre of grasse,
My syth thy stalk before hers come may passe.
Pilgr. Wilt thou provide it may. *Time.* No.
          Pilgr. Alleage the cause.
Time. Because Time cannot alter but obey Fates laws.
Cho. Then happy those whom Fate, that is the stronger,
Together twists their threads, & yet draws hers
    the longer.

The final line twists this dainty argument into a conceit that incorporates the thought and feeling of the whole poem with a suggestion of the sinewy strength of Donne. Between this and one of Marvell's dialogues the difference is one of degree rather than of kind. Place this verse by the side of Waller's *Rose* or Herrick's *Corinna* and you will see how much more it invites the mind and recalls the emotion of Marvell's *Coy Mistress*, which, unlike the other two, does not derive from the simple melancholy of a Catullian lament. Townshend's emotion, though slight by the side of Donne's, shares the Metaphysical reaches which, to use Townshend's phrase,

> for their peculiar ends,
> Hard by Loues cradle build their tombe.

In both sacred and profane verse Donne had revealed this transformation of sensibility, whose imaginative bias is preserved as much in his dramatic taking of the shroud as in the cast of Metaphysical poetry.

Townshend was also capable of following Donne in the use of abstractions to set forth the subtleties of love; for instance, in this stanza from *Pure Simple Love*:

Though thanckfull hands and eyes may prove
    Cyphers of love,
 Yett, till some figure bee prefixt,
As oos, by thousands or alone,
    Stand all for none,
 So, till our lookes and smiles bee mixt
With further meaning, they amount
To nothing by a just account.

This is a typical figure of the Donne sort, for it employs a minor term of neutral imaginative value and retards our imaginative sympathy long enough to bring out the exact curve of the feeling. For a more individual use of the conceit we must look to Townshend's metaphors of the sea.

Upon Kinde and True Love, which Grierson includes in his *Metaphysical Poetry*, shows the harbor metaphor that is Townshend's favorite and best figure. For instance, this passage:

  Let others dote upon her eyes,
  And burn their hearts for sacrifice,
  Beauty's a calm where danger lyes.

  But Kinde and True have been long tried
  A harbour where we may confide,
  And safely there at anchor ride.

Beside this fine passage from one of his finest poems, let us put two stanzas from his poem "*Though regions farr devided.*"

  See then my last lamenting.
   Upon a cliffe I'le sitt,
  Rock Constancy presenting,
   Till I grow part of itt;

My teares a quicksand ffeeding,
Wher on noe ffoote can rest,
My sighs a tempest breeding
About my stony breast.

Those armes, wherin wide open
Loues fleete was wont to putt,
Shall layd acrosse betoken
That havens mouth is shutt.
Myne eyes noe light shall cherish
For shipps att sea distrest,
But darkèling let them perish
Or splitt against my breast.

The last four lines contain what seems to me the
finest conceit in Townshend, his most individual and
arresting use of all the Metaphysical powers of this
figure; and he employs it to give a new prospect of
strangeness to the psychology of love. For me the
harbor metaphor of these two stanzas is sufficient to
establish Townshend's claim to *Kinde and True Love*,
which has been questioned — especially when I feel
in these and other places involving the sea the very
beat of his originality in its deeper notes. Elsewhere
he excels in pastoral images.

I think we may say that Townshend has his place
among the Metaphysical poets and his own little
niche of individual talent. The pleasing tinkle of his
verse, sometimes deepening at the thought of the
sea, is far removed from the iron music of Donne, but
it adds a note to Metaphysical song. His travel in
the employ of Lord Herbert may be faintly reflected
in his verse. While his argumentative passion in
such a poem as *Loves Victory* lacks the complexity of

Donne and approaches more nearly the texture which argument took in the Cavalier lyric, none the less it marks him as an heir of Donne.

These conclusions, properly qualified to the individual, could also be drawn for Kynaston, Godolphin, and Hall. This list might be enlarged from Professor Saintsbury's fine edition of *Caroline Poets*. The first to be added would doubtless be Stanley, whose work is less original because of a veneer which belongs to the polished translator. Except for Cleveland, Benlowes, and Cowley, who do not properly belong in a list of minor Metaphysical poets and so must be discussed later, we should not miss much talent in the Donne tradition down to Cowley if we were to close our list with Stanley. Quarles is not genuinely Metaphysical: he continues the Elizabethan fashion of religious verse and adds Herbert's cult of the emblem. For these reasons, the inclusion of Townshend as a representative minor Metaphysical seems best to achieve my purpose, which is to define the nature of Donne's influence on poets who give continuity to his tradition.[1] To include all the minor figures would be to multiply details and destroy emphasis, rather than to add truth to our perspective.

No one can say that Townshend is the worse poet for being Metaphysical; in fact, one may even doubt whether a man like John Hall would have been a poet, had it not been for the power of the Donne tradition in particular and the Caroline afflatus in

1. For selections from these poets see Grierson's *Metaphysical Poetry*.

general. As Kynaston, turning from rather ordinary
heroic poetry to his first lyric, is at once swept away
by the Caroline conceit and the Caroline cadence, so
the best in Godolphin inclines him also toward the
strain of Donne. The magic of the Caroline cadence
in these poets provokes a hazardous critical question:
Was it Donne or Jonson, or the spirit of the age, that
gave us this marvellous cadence? But this question
will have to wait for an answer. However, we notice
that Townshend has the cadence, along with a peculiar note of his own. For that matter, Townshend
provokes all the questions which apply to a minor
figure in this tradition; but above these he invites
and satisfies a special interest in his individual
talent.

VII. THE CHIEF OFFENDERS

✂✂

JOHN CLEVELAND

CLEVELAND, like Benlowes, is commonly regarded as little more than an awful example of the Metaphysical style. What Butler did for Benlowes, Dryden accomplished pretty effectively for Cleveland — consigned him to the limbo of the abstruse and the grotesque. Posterity has since allowed them even less than the "Character of a Small Poet." However, one editor of Cleveland, Mr. Berdan, has been able to admire him enough to regard him as "the last and most representative of the Metaphysicals." [1] This, I confess, is revenge at a price we cannot afford to pay. For it is true that Cleveland must be numbered among the chief offenders on the side of Metaphysical license — offenders that include Benlowes and Cowley.

Cleveland is in fact one of the "fantastic postillers in song" whom he himself satirizes in *The Hecatomb to his Mistress*: he is a glosser of Metaphysical scripture. He plays the game of conceits as Donne played it in *The Flea*, and he never really gets beyond this witty conceiting, except now and then in his satires. In his amatory verse he is without any genuine feeling; hence, his sole concern is to outdo his rivals in the game of conceits, for which he has a rather pretty

1. *The Poems of John Cleveland*, p. 58.

hand. Nowhere does he play this game more prettily than in *Upon Phillis* or in *The Senses' Festival*. But in this game many reminiscences of Donne appear: for instance, in *The Hecatomb to his Mistress*, the device of defining by negatives,

> As, then, a purer substance is defined
> But by a heap of negatives combined,

or the passage,

> Call her the Metaphysics of her sex,
> And say she tortures wits as quartans vex
> Physicians; call her the square circle; say
> She is the very rule of Algebra.

Besides the levity in the conceits of this poem, there is more than a hint that Cleveland is consciously burlesquing the Metaphysical style as it had degenerated in unskilful hands. But the rest of his verse shows that he did not reject the Donne tradition, though he probably wrote in it with a sly wink at what he regarded as the incompetence of its heirs.

Other reminiscences of Donne have been pointed out in Cleveland. In *The Senses' Festival* there is the parallel, which Professor Gordon has noted, between the passage containing

> When bodies join and victory hovers
> 'Twixt the equal fluttering lovers,

and Donne's lines in *The Extasie*,

> As 'twixt two equall Armies, Fate
> Suspends uncertaine victorie,
> Our soules (which to advance their state
> Were gone out,) hung 'twixt her, and mee.

In the same poem there is an echo of "love's compasses" from Donne's *Valediction*; and in *The Antiplatonic* there is the lesson of Donne's early philosophy, already noted by Professor Saintsbury, in lines like

> Virtue's no more in womankind
> But the green-sickness of the mind.

Fuscara itself is merely a dainty rendering of the Metaphysical manner of Donne's *Elegies*; though pretty, it is probably Cleveland's worst card-castle of wit, supporting nothing but its own rather labored prettiness.

The absence of any serious emotion in Cleveland's verse, other than his satire, leads one to doubt, as Professor Saintsbury has doubted, whether Cleveland ever wrote "serious" verse in one sense at all.[1] His true bent lay in satire, into which he put his heart, though with partial success; he wrote amatory verse in the spirit of one who plays a game, and knows he plays it cleverly and to the liking of his age; with the result that, lacking emotion, his love poems seem to caricature their own cleverness. *The Hecatomb to his Mistress* lends cogent support to this impression, both in its explicit statements and in the nature of its verse. As if to settle all doubt, *The Rebel Scot*, his most famous satire, surprises us with its passion and vigor; its conceits, lashed by the force of his fury, crush his opponents with fantastic abuse. It is significant that there is in Cleveland not a single one of

1. Saintsbury, *Caroline Poets*, iii, 7.

the poignant lyric flights which charm us in the least of the Metaphysicals and beguile the critical sense of the most determined haters of the conceit. The truth is that Cleveland, like the bee in his *Fuscara*, is a confectioner of conceits in his amatory verse, and therefore not an inheritor of the most characteristic Donne manner, but rather of the Italian cast which that manner received at the hands of Crashaw. For no other reason does his verse, when it is praised, receive the epithet "pretty." This of course does not apply to his satire, which uses the conceit in the more genuine Donne manner.

The peculiar talent of Cleveland seems to lie in his skill with the witty image and phrase. Here he puts the heritage from Donne to individual use. On this score a stanza in his verses *To Julia* seems to me the finest thing in Cleveland:

> The candidates of Peter's chair
> Must plead grey hair,
> And use the simony of a cough
> To help them off.
> But when I woo, thus old and spent,
> I'll wed by will and testament.
> No, let us love while crisped and curled;
> The greatest honours, on the agéd hurled,
> Are but gay furloughs for another world.

When Cleveland writes in this vein he exercises his finest talent and points the wit of Donne in the direction of Dryden. At least two poets in his age took occasion to steal witty conceits of this sort from him:

they were Marvell and Vaughan. I might add Benlowes, but he must be examined presently.

Vaughan has been condemned for the one which he
stole, because some have felt that he was following
Herbert's way of using images.[1] Actually, he was
simply trying to remake one of Cleveland's in the
verses *Upon Phillis*:

> The marigold (whose courtier's face
> Echoes the sun and doth unlace
> Her at his rise — at his full stop
> Packs and shuts up her gaudy shop)
> Mistakes her cue and doth display.

Here is Vaughan in *Faith*:

> But as in Nature when the day
>   Breaks, night adjourns,
> Stars shut up shop, mists pack away
>   And the moon mourns.

Cleveland printed his in 1647, and Vaughan his in
1650. Two things strike us in this comparison: first,
that Cleveland's conceit is one of excellent wit; and
second, that Vaughan's is a failure because he tries to
fuse an essentially witty image into a highly imaginative context involving a serious emotion. While
Vaughan's image is less serious than he intended it to
be, Cleveland's is exactly what he intended it, a witty
compliment to Phillis.

One of the images in *Appleton House* for which
Marvell has often been reprimanded is this:

1. See Beeching's Introduction to *Vaughan*, Muses' Library, pp.
xl–xli.

But now the *Salmon-Fishers* moist
Their *Leathern Boats* begin to hoist;
And, like *Antipodes* in Shoes,
Have shod their *Heads* in their *Canoos*.[1]

Three years before these lines were written Cleveland had printed his *Square-Cap*, which contains the same image:

Then Calot Leather-cap strongly pleads,
   And fain would derive the pedigree of fashion.
The antipodes wear their shoes on their heads,
   And why may not we in their imitation?

As a witty argument to the Cambridge lass who would have no man but a Square-cap, this is more successful, certainly, than as an image to mark the coming of night in *Appleton House*. In Marvell it is gratuitous, it supports nothing but its own cleverness; in Cleveland it is all the poor lawyer has to stand on in his argument for favor. The source of its failure in Marvell is the introduction of *Canoos*, which brings the image into Dr. Johnson's class of "enormous and disgusting hyperboles." [2] Thus it appears that Cleveland was sometimes a better man than his debtors, that he had a certain skill in the witty image that is not to be despised.

On the metrical side Cleveland has excited interest because of the apparently deliberate use of trisyllabic rhythm in poems like *Square-Cap* and *Mark Antony*. Whether he owed the rhythm to the much-

1. Margoliouth, *Marvell's Poems and Letters*, i, 83.
2. Professor Margoliouth also notes this parallel, but makes no comment, *op. cit.*, i, 235.

disputed first line of Donne's *Twickenham Garden*
one cannot say, but one can scarcely deny that his
use is conscious and deliberate. Perhaps less conscious and more in accord with the inclination of the
time is the way in which his couplet is getting on
toward Dryden. The Donne tradition and the fore-
shadowed tradition of Dryden meet in Cleveland's
Elegy upon the Archbishop of Canterbury; the new
voice may be heard in the first couplet:

> I need no Muse to give my passion vent,
> He brews his tears that studies to lament.

Even the crushing contempt of Dryden surprises us
in a couplet like that at the close of *The Antiplatonic*:

> Like an ambassador that beds a queen
> With the nice caution of a sword between.

We may conclude that Cleveland's peculiar talent
lay in phrasing, in the phrase or image that kills,
vents wit, or is pretty; and that this talent was con-
siderably indebted to the Donne tradition. But
Cleveland lacked the poetic or lyric reach of Benlowes, with whom he may be profitably compared.

EDWARD BENLOWES

Of all the Metaphysical poets Benlowes is probably
the most fantastic. His *Theophila*, published in 1652,
is in appearance the most learned poem of this school.
But with all its fantastic qualities and its awkward
metrics, it has a glowing intensity that is far from the
prose and sense we saw creeping into Cleveland.

Theophila — named for the soul as the bride of Christ — is a remarkable example of the superb religious verse of the seventeenth century. It is as remarkable for a profound sense of the immense space which surrounds human life — only matched in that century by Donne and Milton — as for what could happen to Metaphysical poetry when it packed all of its extravagance into one mind. It is truly a catch-all of the Donne tradition, burned into poetry by the undoubted *furor poeticus* of Edward Benlowes.

To get the measure of Benlowes we may as well begin by comparing him to Cleveland, of whom there are not a few echoes in *Theophila*. One echo, already noticed by Professor Saintsbury, is from these lines in *The Senses' Festival*:[1]

> Not the fair Abbess of the skies,
> With all her nunnery of eyes,
> Can show me such a glorious prize!

Here is Benlowes a year later:

> That lady-prioress of the cloister'd sky,
>   Coach'd with her spangled vestals nigh,
> Vails to this constellation from divinity.[2]

Having more of the suggestiveness of true poetry, Benlowes is, I believe, the more poetic of the two. The borrowing from Cleveland here suggested gains support from the passage in *Theophila* from which

---

1. See *Caroline Poets*, vol. iii, notes to p. 19. Saintsbury is uncertain which way the indebtedness went; this caution is unnecessary, for Benlowes was a great borrower.

2. *Ibid.*, i, 356; Canto III, stanza xliii.

this is taken. Only a few stanzas away we find this image:

> (Pearl'd dews add stars) Yet earth's shade shuts up soon
>   Her shop of beams; whose cone doth run
> 'Bove th' horned moon, beneath the golden-tressèd sun.[1]

This is yet another reworking of the 'marigold' conceit from Cleveland, and much more successful than Vaughan's. Other echoes could be adduced if time permitted. However, the reader may content himself with respect to the catch-all character of *Theophila* by turning to Canto IV, which is a veritable thesaurus of Metaphysical verse.

Just before the passage from which I last quoted we may read one of the finest passages in Benlowes:

> But, might we her sweet breast, Love's Eden, see;
>   On those snow-mountlets apples be,
> May cure those mischiefs wrought by the forbidden tree.
>
> Her hands are soft, as swanny down, and much
>   More white; whose temperate warmth is such,
> As when ripe gold and quick'ning sunbeams inly touch.
>
> Ye sirens of the groves, who, perch'd on high,
>   Tune gutt'ral sweets, air-minstrels, why
> From your bough-cradles, rock'd with wind, to Her d' ye fly?
>
> See, lilies, gown'd in tissue, simper by her;
>   With marigolds in flaming tire;
> Green satin'd bays, with primrose fringed, seem all on fire.[2]

This is the sensuous embodiment of the soul, Theophila the bride of Christ. As in Herbert, it represents

---

1. Saintsbury, *op. cit.*, i, 356.
2. *Ibid.*, p. 355.

the tendency to give religion a sensuous habitation, and therefore it would offend Courthope by the materialism of its images. But for this very reason, it is characteristic of the age and dependent for its strength upon the Donne tradition. Otherwise, it might be religious verse, not poetry.

But Theophila has another form for Benlowes; in certain states of mind she becomes a mystical figure:

'T was at Night's noon, when sleep th' oppressed had
    drown'd;
  But sleepless were oppressors found;
'T was when Sky's spangled head in sable veil was bound:

For thievish Night had stole, and clos'd up quite,
  In her dark lantern, starry light:
No planet seen to sail in that dead ebb of Night:

When, lo, all-spreading rays the room surround!
  Like such reflections, as rebound,
Shooting their beams to th' sun, from rocks of diamond.

This, to a wonder, summonèd my sight,
  Which dazzled was at so pure light!
A Form angelic there appear'd divinely bright! [1]

Such mystical devotion, invested in the manner of Vaughan, brings us the other side of seventeenth-century religious feeling, so glowing in its intensity. Once more we are with Donne "at the round earths imagin'd corners," or left alone with Vaughan's Lampe, while we listen to the fantastic music of Benlowes' devotion. Especially is the sense of immense space present in this fifth canto, though barely hinted in such a stanza as

1. Saintsbury, *op. cit.*, i, 370.

Chime out, ye crystal spheres, and tune your poles;
    Skies, sound your bass; ere ye to coals
Dissolve, and tumble on the bonfire world in shoals.[1]

In this quality Benlowes is surpassed in his age only by Milton, and perhaps no more than equalled by Donne in his *Anniversaries*. While Benlowes is capable of most of the variations on the conceit which we have found among the Metaphysicals, his most individual use of it resembles Crashaw's in sensuousness, but is less luscious and more astringent.

Despite the fine things in Benlowes, we must not fail to recognize that if he is capable of greater poetic flights than Cleveland, he is not less capable of greater absurdities, not only than Cleveland but also than any other Metaphysical poet. He combines greater extremes of colloquial and learned words, of English and Latin verse, of the ugly contractions which are such a blot on the poetry of this time and the irregular syntax which adds to the obscurity. In short, he represents such license and such afflatus that, beside him, Cleveland seems a disciple of prose and sense. In extravagance of figure the following stanza is certainly not the worst to be found in him:

Betimes, when keen-breath'd winds, with frosty cream,
    Periwig bald trees, glaze tattling stream:
For May-games past, white-sheet *peccavi* is Winter's
    theme.[2]

Although Benlowes made this over from Sylvester,

1. *Ibid.*, p. 371.
2. *Ibid.*, p. 365; Canto IV, stanza lxviii. On the Sylvester source see note to p. 310.

he did not borrow more absurdity than he could
make. For instance, this stanza:

Each gallon breeds a ruby; — drawer! score 'um —
  Cheeks dyed in claret seem o' th' quorum,
When our nose-carbuncles, like link-boys, blaze before 'um.[1]

What shall we say to this? Before we answer, let us
feel the throb of religious emotion invade this fantastic Benlowes.

O prodigy of great and good! Faith, sound
This Love's abyss, that does so strangely bound
Almightiness Itself! From whose veins, see,
Unsluic'd, Love's purple ocean, when His free
Red-streaming life did vanquish Death and Hell!
That thou might'st live, He died! That thou might rise,
  He fell![2]

The glowing intensity of such mystical devotion
forces us to accept the extravagant expression as an
appropriate, even as the necessary, vesture of such a
state of mind. In this acceptance lies much of the
authentic power of seventeenth-century devotional
verse. For this reason Benlowes may be severely reprimanded but never wholly condemned. With all
its eccentricity, *Theophila* contains passages without
which poetry would be the poorer.

It was easy for Butler to make game of Benlowes,
and even now it is difficult to be fair to him. In spite
of Butler's gibe that contact with *Theophila* made one
suffer from a tendency to write harsh poetry, Dryden,

1. Saintsbury, *op. cit.*, i, 336; Canto I, stanza xx.
2. *Ibid.*, pp. 361–362; Canto IV, stanzas xi–xii.

who probably read Benlowes, points the way to a new tradition of smooth poetry. But Cowley, the last of our awful exemplars of the Donne tradition, was already leaning in that direction; in fact, Cleveland himself had anticipated the new voice. From Benlowes, the last believer in the old enthusiasm, we turn to Cowley and the late and frigid note of the Donne tradition among its direct inheritors.

ABRAHAM COWLEY

After describing the style and sentiments of the Metaphysical poets, Dr. Johnson went on to speak of Cowley as "almost the last of that race, and undoubtedly the best." We should agree, I believe, that Cowley was the last of the direct heirs of Donne, but not that he was the best of that race. These were Johnson's words after he had pilloried Cowley for his Metaphysical delinquencies. Milton, we remember, put Cowley with Shakspere and Spenser, although Milton presumably disapproved of the Metaphysicals. In this opinion we get an idea of Cowley's great contemporary reputation, which was unquestioned by anyone but Dryden, and by Dryden only at the end of his life. Cowley first drew fire because of *The Mistress*,[1] his most direct echo of Donne, but not his best tribute of indebtedness.

When Cowley thought of retiring to the country he wrote a preface to justify an edition of his poems.

1. See A. H. Nethercot, "The Reputation of the 'Metaphysical Poets' during the Seventeenth Century," *Jour. Engl. and Ger. Phil.*, xxiii, (1924), 178.

Part of his argument was this: "And I think *Doctor Donnes Sun Dyal in a grave* is not more useless and ridiculous then *Poetry* would be in that *retirement*." It is significant that Cowley's mind forgets its "unequalled fertility of invention" and turns to Donne in this moment, for Donne had been the master of his muse, though Spenser had first turned him to poetry. But let us look at the nature of Cowley's inheritance and the way in which he modified its power.

In one important respect Cowley's mind was like Donne's: it was susceptible to learning, and particularly to the influence of the new science and philosophy. His *Ode to Mr. Hobs* and his *Ode to the Royal Society* are sufficient witnesses of the peculiar skill with which he could figure forth the abstractions of philosophy in the concreteness of poetry. His learning appears everywhere in his poetry and is very apparent in his amatory verse, where it is used in the typical fashion of Donne. Even a casual reading of *The Mistress* will disclose the titles, themes, and images of Donne; the wit, antitheses, and startling introductions; but not the passion, personality, or intense intellectual vigor. Long ago Dr. Johnson observed that one of the stanzas of *Maidenhead* would probably not have been written, had Cowley not remembered Donne's thought in *Loves Alchemie*. The same could be said for other passages in *The Mistress*. But more interesting than actual borrowings are the things which Donne taught Cowley.

First, there is the skill in analysis. Certainly, Cowley's poem *Against Hope* would not be the

triumph of analysis that critics since Johnson have
felt it to be, if Donne had not first practised this
analytic art. And Cowley's poem *Of Wit*, which attempts to analyze the very secret of Metaphysical
verse, falls back upon definition by negatives, which
Donne had exemplified in *Negative love*. Cowley says,

> What is it then, which like the *Power Divine*
> We only can by *Negatives* define?

where Donne had said,

> If that be simply perfectest
> Which can by no way be exprest
> But *Negatives*, my love is so.

Besides this art of analysis in Cowley, there is the
rational evolution, the lyric argument, which comes
from Donne. Such intellectual structure is found in
poems of Cowley as diverse as *The Change* and *Of Wit*;
even so dainty a thing as *The Chronicle* depends upon
it, as Herrick's chronicle of his mistresses does not.

Moreover, Cowley uses the homely and learned
word and figure of Donne, for Cowley also practices
the conceit; indeed, to Dr. Johnson he was one of the
worst offenders. I think that he was even more fond
than Donne of the expanded conceit; in *Destinie* he
elaborates the figure of a game of chess to the farthest
extent to which ingenuity can carry it, and so lays
himself open to the chief condemnation of Dr. Johnson, "that of pursuing his thoughts to their last
ramifications." This is generally a valid criticism of
Cowley, for his conceits rarely succeed, like Donne's,
by throwing a new or unusual light on the psychology

of feeling. When they do succeed, it is usually by a
triumph of ingenuity, of sheer intellectual agility,
such as that which conquered Dr. Johnson's objections to poems like *Against Hope* and *Of Wit*. Cowley's fondness for the expanded conceit impresses us
when we notice that it provides a pattern for verses
like *The Chronicle* or like *The Duel* in the *Anacreontiques*. A rather typical conceit of the commoner sort
may be found in the *Elegie upon Anacreon*:

> *Love* was with thy *Life* entwin'd
> Close as *Heat* with *Fire* is joyn'd,
> A powerful *Brand* prescrib'd the date
> Of thine, like *Meleagers* Fate.
> Th' *Antiperistasis* of *Age*
> More enflam'd thy amorous rage.

This is ingenious, but somehow it lacks the intellectual vigor, the agitated mind of Donne, whose conceits can seldom be called merely ingenious. The
contortions of Donne's mind were never so easy, so
frictionless and therefore devoid of heat.

This difference in Cowley's mind, together with
his lack of passion, probably accounts for his greatest
gift, the light touch of his wit, his levity. Nowhere
does this wit shine to greater advantage than in the
Anacreontiques, in the verses on *Drinking* or in the
lines which end *The Account*:

> There's a whole *Map* behind of *Names*.
> Of gentle Love i' th' *temperate Zone*,
> And cold ones in the *Frigid One*,
> Cold frozen *Loves* with which I pine,
> And parched *Loves* beneath the *Line*.

Here the conceit and the levity are one in an alliance so sparkling with dry wit that we feel none could have achieved it but Cowley. When learning comes to the aid of his levity, he gives us wit like that which points his second poem on the *Epicure*:

> After *Death* I nothing crave,
> Let me *Alive* my pleasures have,
> All are *Stoicks* in the *Grave*.

This is the happiest sort of learned wit, and may have been suggested by "*Doctor Donnes Sun Dyal in a grave*," which Cowley spoke of in his Preface. However, a comparison of the conceit in Cowley with the conceit in Donne reveals the different talents of the two poets pretty clearly: the plangency and dark emotion of Donne's conceit contrast sharply with the dry point and gay malice of Cowley's. The *discordia concors*, or imaginative distance, in both is peculiar to Metaphysical wit, and should not be confused with the antithetical wit of balanced form which comes in with the next age, typically in Dryden's words on Doeg:

> A double noose thou on thy neck dost pull
> For writing treason and for writing dull.

Metaphysical wit is inherent in the fibre of the thought; it often appears cynical because it carries the rebuke of reason to the emotions; it is toughly intellectual because it is created by a tension between reason and knowledge. But it can be highly imaginative and profoundly moving in its revelation.

To be such it must be born in an agitated mind, which Cowley seldom knew.

And yet there were things which moved Cowley: as well as by the loss of his friends and the promise of mild country joys, he was moved, even to wistfulness, by the hope of literary immortality. With more than usual emotion and with a sceptical, melancholy music seldom heard in him, he puts the enigmatic question with which his *Miscellanies* open:

> What shall I do to be for ever known,
> And make the *Age to come* my own?

This emotion, together with his brilliant analytic skill, seems to account for one of his finest poems, *Against Hope*. Popularity did not turn Cowley's head, but seems rather to have instilled into him the lingering doubt that perhaps he might not, after all, be remembered. It is this emotion and this doubt that give animus to his poem *Against Hope*, in which his brilliant analysis reflects a mood like that of *Ecclesiastes*. Crashaw's answer to this poem gives us an admirable opportunity of measuring Cowley against another Metaphysical poet, who was farther from the new tradition of Dryden.

Let us take a parallel stanza from each poem. Here is the third in Cowley:

> *Hope*, Fortunes cheating *Lottery*!
> Where for one *prize* an hundred *blanks* there be;
> Fond *Archer*, *Hope*, who tak'st thy aim so far,
> That still or *short*, or *wide* thine arrows are!

Thin, empty *Cloud*, which th'eye deceives
With shapes that our own *Fancy* gives!
A *Cloud*, which gilt and painted now appears,
But must drop presently in *tears*!
When thy false beams o're *Reasons* light prevail,
By *Ignes fatui* for *North-Stars* we sail.

And here is the parallel in Crashaw's *Answer for Hope*:

Fair hope! our earlyer heav'n by thee
Young time is taster to eternity.
Thy generous wine with age growes strong, not sowre.
Nor does it kill thy fruit, to smell thy flowre.
Thy golden, growing, head never hangs down
Till in the lappe of loves full noone
It falls; and dyes! o no, it melts away
As does the dawn into the day.
As lumpes of sugar lose themselves; and twine
Their supple essence with the soul of wine.

In the first place, it is obvious that Cowley's wit is like champagne, dry and sparkling; while Crashaw's is like a liqueur, full and perfumed. Both are Metaphysical, and both represent a development by rapid association of thought. But there is this great difference: Cowley develops his thought by quick strokes which are discontinuous; Crashaw develops his by forcing connections on his first figure that are not implicit but that acquire continuity in the web of the thought. Cowley's development has its parallel in Donne's *Canonization*, while Crashaw's development goes back to Donne's *Valediction: of weeping*, which certainly represents Donne's most

individual way of thinking. But either Cowley or
Crashaw was capable of the manner of developing
thought which the other has used in this instance, as
the rest of each poem suggests. Although Crashaw
has written the finer poetry, I think we must admit
that Cowley has achieved the greater triumph of
ingenuity, of brilliant analysis, but not without be-
traying some of the emotion with which he thought
of "the strange witchcraft of Anon!"

Certain larger conclusions which may be drawn
from this comparison show us the fate that was over-
taking Metaphysical poetry. While Cowley's wit is
still Metaphysical, it is less extravagant, and less
passionate and imaginative, than Crashaw's. The
intensity of Donne is passing away in Cowley, and
the long struggle between reason and imagination is
coming to a close in the victory of reason and good
sense. The general sensibility of the age has come to
be represented more by Mr. Hobbes and the Royal
Society than by Dr. Donne and religious struggle.
Cowley, who was outside of the older sensibility in
his political life, was likewise out of it in his poetic
life; hence his wit, though attracted to the Donne
tradition, never reflects the passionate, intellectual,
and mystical conception of life and love and death
which Donne and his disciples held. But the cool dry
intelligence of Cowley appealed to the new sensibility
and prepared the way for the greater genius of Dryden.

This preparation has two sides. The loss of passion and imagination which poetry suffered from this

change in sensibility Cowley tried to repair by making poetry eloquent, as well as witty. Out of the high style of the Elizabethans, the seventeenth century, in T. S. Eliot's brilliant generalization, separated two qualities: wit and magniloquence.[1] This separation first becomes clear in Cowley; this was his great service to Dryden. Cowley's wit we have already noticed as the chief quality of some of his best verse. His magniloquence is the most striking quality of his *Pindarique Odes*; it never reaches a higher level than in this passage in the *Ode to Mr. Hobs*:

> Long did the mighty *Stagirite* retain
> The *universal Intellectual reign*,
> Saw his own Countreys short-liv'ed *Leopard* slain;
> The stronger *Roman-Eagle* did out-fly,
> Oftner *renewed* his *Age*, and saw that *Dy*.
> *Mecha* it self, in spite of *Mahumet* possest,
> And chas'ed by a wild *Deluge* from the *East*,
> His *Monarchy* new planted in the *West*.

Thus did Cowley prepare for poetry's ascent to the rostrum, for the heroic drama and *Religio Laici*. Even in his most moving poems, *On the Death of Mr. William Hervey* and *On the Death of Mr. Crashaw*, one feels that if he were giving less undisturbed attention to the reality of human sorrow, he could easily slip into the large utterance that forgets to inspect the human heart.

Thus reason and eloquence came to rule in Cowley's verse. Dryden was to improve the eloquence and change the form of wit which reason took; but he

1. See Eliot's *Homage to John Dryden*, p. 35.

was not to match Cowley in the wit which is still Metaphysical in form, if not altogether in feeling. To this wit Cowley gave a dry bouquet and gay malice which corresponded to his adroit and supple mind, and informed his best verse with its finest and most individual quality. The levity of the *Anacreontiques* and the subtle analysis of the odes on *Wit* and *Hope* are not only Cowley's highest tribute to the Donne tradition, but they are also the things most likely to make him "for ever known."

VIII. THE FRINGE OF THE TRADITION

THE FRINGE of the Donne tradition, which means primarily the Cavalier poets, is best elucidated by its contact with Ben Jonson. For his influence on these poets, whether by direct indebtedness or by persuasion to classical models, unites with that of Donne to form the Caroline lyric. To their contemporaries there was nothing antithetical in the poetic ideals of the two men. On the other hand, there were complementary qualities, as well as common qualities, in each that combined in the Cavalier school to give us a kind of song that is unique in English poetry. Moreover, it is probable that Jonson himself was influenced by Donne.

This probability involves a quarrel of long standing which relates to the four remarkable elegies on a lover's quarrel and separation printed in Jonson's *Underwoods* as numbers lvii–lx. The reasons for the argument are two: first, *Underwoods* lviii was included in the 1633 edition of Donne; and second, all four elegies have marks of the Donne manner. While Whalley and Gifford both noticed the attribution of one of the elegies to Donne, neither deprived Jonson of the authorship; but Fleay assigned all four to Donne. Swinburne also was inclined to give them to Donne. Chambers and Grierson, retaining the one already printed as Donne's, paid no attention to the others. Herford and Simpson, the last editors of Jonson, join Fleay and Swinburne in giving all four elegies to Donne. Professor W. D. Briggs, in reviewing Herford and Simpson's work, advances cogent arguments for assigning the four elegies to Jonson.[1] One thing seems to me certain: not to consider these elegies as a group must be fatal to any attribution of authorship, for all are limited by one subject and one style. This style Professor Briggs thinks that of an imitator of Donne, and I believe rightly.

The main force of the argument urged by Professor Briggs lies in the discovery that these elegies borrow from Catullus, Ovid, Seneca, and probably Tibullus and Propertius.[2] Such borrowing is characteristic of Jonson, but not of Donne, in whom Grierson can trace with certainty only Ovid, Horace, and Juvenal. Professor Briggs also establishes an interesting parallel with the *Discoveries*. However, in Elegy lix there is an echo of Donne's figure of the compasses; but Jonson had already borrowed this — as Gifford noticed — in his verses to Selden, *Underwoods* xxxi. Professor Herford admits that "Jonson did not indeed altogether fail to attempt" the Propertian sort of elegy in which Donne was so great,[3] as there are two other unusual elegies in *Underwoods*, "*Can beauty, that did prompt me first to write*" (xxxv)

1. See *Modern Language Notes*, vol. xlii, no. 6 (June, 1927), pp. 409–410.
2. See also his article on Jonson's indebtedness to the classics, *Modern Philology*, xv (September, 1917), 85–120.
3. Herford and Simpson, *Ben Jonson*, ii, 388.

and *"By those bright eyes, at whose immortal fires"* (xxxvi). But the facts are even stronger, since both elegies are full of echoes from Elegy xii of Donne, *His parting from her*: the former has the ingenious play between Love and Fortune, and the latter the central situation of a lady with a husband, while both echo many of the turns of thought in Donne. This indebtedness is not surprising, for we know from Drummond's *Conversations* that Jonson had Donne's Elegy xi by heart: "his verses of the Lost Chaine he hath by heart." [1]

The problem of imitation or attribution is further complicated by the two poems which follow these two elegies in the *Underwoods*. They are the two Satirical Shrubs which Gifford recognized as more in the style and manner of Donne than of Jonson, though he did not settle the authorship. These poems have more of the strange dark mood of Donne than we find in the two elegies. The next poem in *Underwoods* is the rather fine elegy in the *In Memoriam* stanza. This, Herford admits, "has much of Donne's close intellectual texture, but without his sudden splendours and his pervading glow." [2] And Herford is perfectly right, for the manner of developing thought in this elegy is characteristic of Donne but not of Jonson. Moreover, is not the lack of sudden splendors and pervading glow exactly what we should expect from an imitation of Donne by Jon-

1. Gifford-Cunningham, *Works of Ben Jonson*, iii, 474.
2. *Op. cit.*, ii, 388. In Jonson's *Silent Woman* there is a likely allusion to *The Autumnall*, Elegy ix. See Grierson, *Donne's Poetical Works*, ii, 63.

son? It is just in such respects that all these poems in *Underwoods* betray the hand of an imitator of Donne; even the four remarkable elegies grow pale beside the authentic elegies of Donne. And yet we must admit that here Jonson caught much of the spirit, as well as of the manner and style, of Donne. The evidence seems strong for the conclusion that Jonson by imitating Donne here achieved the genuine accents of passion which he caught in song perhaps once, in *"Drink to me only with thine eyes."* I do not see how we can avoid concluding that Jonson, who knew some of Donne's verses by heart, was himself a follower of Donne in the poems which I have mentioned. It is no more than we should expect from one who esteemed Donne so highly, and who gave him the part of Criticus in his lost preface to the *Art of Poetry*.

Jonson's imitation of Donne was assisted by a fundamental kinship between the two poets, which existed despite their differences. What Jonson imitated in Donne was of course what he lacked, but not something that was antithetical to his poetic ideals. In their different ways each challenged the great Spenserian tradition of facile and melting verse. Did Jonson not tell Drummond that "Spenser's stanzas pleased him not, nor his matter?" [1] Both stood for a masculine line in poetry, weighty, concentrated, and astringent. Both sought to make poetry more intellectual, to incorporate their erudition into their sensibility, though their wit and their erudition were different. And both gave poetic language a simple and

1. Gifford-Cunningham, *op. cit.*, iii, 470.

vital directness of speech. The astonishing daring of Donne's images is not born of the impulse to decorate, but of the impulse to leap straight to the heart of his matter. While passion burned away the dross for Donne, the labor of the file did the same for Jonson; and so each, by different paths, arrived at the same end.

To the achievement of these ideals Donne brought his extraordinary but wayward genius, and Jonson his fine controlling hand of art. Donne, the strange explorer of the soul, contrasts with Jonson, the savage cartoonist of life who could sometimes be a little sorry for a vanished child or friend; and yet they were brothers in poetry, though Jonson might chasten the extravagance and rough accents of Donne, and Donne might subdue his critical friend by the very power of his fiery and daring genius. A more haunting music comes out of Donne, but Jonson was capable of a meditative eloquence and a fugitive sweetness; yet both triumph over the natural astringency of their verse. Though Donne is commonly regarded as the rougher of the two, Swinburne apparently thought Jonson inferior to Donne, for he says:

Donne is rugged: Jonson is stiff. And if ruggedness of verse is a damaging blemish, stiffness of verse is a destructive infirmity. Ruggedness is curable; witness Donne's *Anniversaries*: stiffness is incurable; witness Jonson's *Underwoods*.[1]

Swinburne goes on to say that *The Forest* and *Underwoods* have every quality but the peculiar magic of

1. *A Study of Ben Jonson*, p. 99.

poetry. I believe that Swinburne is quite right in
this judgment; and surely no one would deny that,
whatever Donne's defects, he has the peculiar magic
of poetry, which is not the same as romantic glamour.
Though Jonson may have the better versification,
Donne has the more haunting tune. And in contrast
Donne's erudition is primarily medieval, and Jonson's
is classical; while Donne's wit is "metaphysical," and
Jonson's is closer to that of the Latin lyrists. These
are their principal differences.

There are some special differences between the
lyric verse of Jonson and that of Donne which we
must distinguish for our remarks on the fringe of the
Donne tradition. The first of these refers to the
structure of the lyric. One of the most striking
traits of Donne's lyric is, as we have seen, its argument, its dialectic of passion, its close intellectual
structure. Now Professor Herford finds that the
temper of dialectic could seriously impair the execu-
tion of a charming lyric motive in Jonson.[1] For an
example he points to the stanzas called *A Nymph's
Passion*. Here is the first stanza:

> I love, and he loves me again,
>   Yet dare I not tell who;
> For if the nymphs should know my swain,
>   I fear they'd love him too;
>   Yet if it be not known,
>   The pleasure is as good as none,
> For that's a narrow joy is but our own.

But this poem has not the tough evolution of thought

1. *Op. cit.*, ii, 390.

which marks Donne, and which Professor Herford found reflected in the elegy "*Though beauty be the mark of praise.*" Rather it is a fairly simple dilemma, and not even comparable to the fundamental brain work of a song like Donne's "*Sweetest love, I do not goe,*" which has a much more continuous chain of thought and a tougher dialectic of passion. Moreover, such argument is the exception in Jonson, while it is the rule in Donne.

No less different is Jonson's use of the conceit. When we come across a conceit of the Donne sort in Jonson, like the compasses in the verses to Selden and in Elegy lix, it is with a distinct shock. For we recognize that Jonson's typical conceit is like that of the Greek Anthology and the Latin lyrists, the sort we find in "*Drink to me only with thine eyes,*" the *Celia* and the *Charis* poems; it is not subtly intellectual. But Jonson's wit is similar to Donne's: it has the same intellectual basis, the same alliance of levity and seriousness, which we find also in Catullus; it lacks, however, that touch of the fantastic which characterizes the wit of Donne. In all of these differences we may observe the strong hand of classical restraint in Jonson.

In one respect Jonson seems to have learned less than Donne from the Latin poets. That is in urbanity and the art of amatory verse. I do not forget the savage and dark emotion in Donne, for we have that also in Catullus. But Jonson, especially in his attitude to women, reveals a savage and rather blunt cynicism that is further from urbanity and sophisticated wit than the normal disposition of Donne. Badinage and mocking worldliness were much more native to the temperament of Donne than to that of Jonson. Unfair though it may be, compare Jonson's *Conversations* with Donne's *Letters*. Donne could be grossly indelicate, but he possessed greater finesse than Jonson. All of these qualities appear in Donne's amatory verse, where they produce the mocking philosophy of a man of the world, except when they are profoundly disrupted by the *"Odi et amo"* of Catullus. I cannot imagine Jonson capable of the gesture with which Donne met one of the greatest disappointments of his life. You remember that upon losing his secretaryship, because of his marriage, he sent to his wife that famous postscript, "John Donne, Anne Donne, Un-done." Even the urbanity mixed with so much levity and so much seriousness would have been beyond the reach of Ben Jonson in similar circumstances. Both the serious and the light side of Donne's worldly philosophy will be important in our discussion of the Cavalier school.

To his contemporaries Jonson was the king of verse just as Donne was the king of wit. This is a common tribute from the eulogists of *Jonsonus Virbius*, who praise Jonson chiefly for his learning and his art. Mayne, who wrote an elegy for Donne, calls Jonson the "prince of numbers." Bishop King reveals a common attitude when he speaks of Jonson as the teacher of his age. Here we realize the difference in the fame of the two poets: Jonson is praised for his learning and laborious art and for the tribute which he levied upon the Greek and Latin poets, where Donne was praised for his soaring wit, intense genius, and striking originality. Falkland shows us that Jonson's songs were regarded for "their enchanting power," and King eulogizes the purity of his language. Carew's lines *To Ben Jonson* help along Jonson's reputation for laborious art,

> Repine not at the taper's thrifty waste,
> That sleeks thy terser poems,

and also convince me that Carew meant Jonson when, in his elegy to Donne, he spoke of "the subtle cheat of slie Exchanges" with the classics. It seems pretty clear that to a man like Carew, Jonson was the schoolmaster, and Donne the genius, of Caroline verse. Of course Jonson was a master of extraordinary talent. A lively light is thrown over the position of Jonson by a letter which James Howell wrote to Sir Thomas Hawk on April 5, 1636:

I was invited yesternight to a solemn supper by B. J., where you were deeply remembered; there was good company, excellent cheer, choice wines, and jovial welcome: one thing intervened, which almost spoiled the relish of the rest, that B. began to engross all the discourse, to vapour extremely of himself and by vilifying others to magnify his own Muse. T. Ca. buzzed me in the ear, that though Ben had barrelled up a great deal of knowledge, yet it seems he had not read the *Ethics*, which, among other Precepts of Morality, forbid Self-commendation.

T. Ca. is Thomas Carew, and this James Howell praised Jonson in *Jonsonus Virbius* for his "strenuous lines."

From this comparison of Jonson and Donne it is not hard to see why Donne contributed more to the Cavalier school than Jonson. For one thing, we must remember that the Cavalier poets could hear in Donne the authentic voice of love, which they could never quite hear in Jonson, though they might hear some of its accents. The influences which moulded the Cavalier school were no doubt three: Donne, Jonson, the Latin and Greek lyrists; and of these the chief was Donne. If we may define the spheres of such influence, Donne was their inspiration and genius, Jonson was their master of versification, and the classical lyrists were their examples in ancient tradition. In the fundamental brain work and sophistication of the Caroline lyric, which distinguish it from the Elizabethan lyric, the influence of Donne is perhaps the stronger; but in purity of language and prosody the influence of Jonson is the stronger. The definite contribution of Donne to the Cavalier school was threefold: first, the passionate paradoxical argument, the dialectic of passion; second, the Caroline conceit; and third, the worldly philosophy of gallantry and devotion. One might add a certain hardness of line. All of these qualities were diluted in the Caroline lyric by the modifying influence of Jonson, who demanded sobriety, classical restraint, and obedience to laws in art. In this curbing influence Jonson was assisted by the example of the Latin and Greek lyrists, though the spirit of these was on the side of Donne. In wit the Cavalier school probably learned from all three influences, not forgetting a touch of the fantastic from Donne.

The Caroline cadence, perhaps the most marvelous quality of all, sings in both Cavalier and Metaphysical verse; but whether Jonson or Donne taught it to the Caroline poets remains a mystery. It is probably to Jonson that we must look for their master in this, for he was their "prince of numbers." If so, the pupils frequently outdid the master. Though Donne often has a haunting tune that Jonson lacks, Jonson has left us more perfect examples of the favorite Caroline tunes, the "common" and the "long" measure. Here is Jonson in the "common" measure:

> Oh do not wanton with those eyes,
> Lest I be sick with seeing;
> Nor cast them down, but let them rise,
> Lest shame destroy their being.

His finest effort in this measure is of course "*Drink to me only with thine eyes.*" Donne used the same measure in his *Undertaking*. The "long" variety of "eights" measure gives us some of Donne's finest poems, *The Extasie, A Valediction: forbidding mourning*, or *A Feaver*; this is the cadence:

> O! Do not die, for I shall hate
> All women so, when thou art gone,
> That thee I shall not celebrate,
> When I remember thou wast one.

The *In Memoriam* variety of "eights" measure is

represented by Lord Herbert's *Ode* and by Jonson's *Elegy*, where it runs thus:

> Though beauty be the mark of praise,
>   And yours of whom I sing be such
>   As not the world can praise too much
> Yet 't is your Virtue now I raise.

Confronted with these samples of the Caroline cadence, we may well wonder who taught it to the poets who often surpassed Jonson himself. The most likely solution, it seems to me, is that Jonson taught them numbers, but Donne gave them the peculiar dash which makes their verse go with such incomparable throb and soar. At any rate, we cannot afford to discount the influence of Donne, who, though rugged, could write such verse as "*Sweetest love, I do not goe.*"

Since Donne was the first to carry argument over into the winged movement of the song, and since this revolution most distinguishes the Caroline lyric from the Elizabethan, I am inclined to believe that his quick intense dialectic of passion is the real source of the Caroline cadence. The weight which this dialectic lays upon the syllables that fall under the metrical stress, and the consequent necessity of rhetorical *addition* to the strict foot-system, give to the Caroline poets their peculiar dash. This grew out of Donne's tendency to stress the *sense* rather than the *sound* of his verse, although he reached his finest music only when passion burned the dross out of his numbers. The contrary tendency is found in Jonson, where the desire for metrical regularity produces

many distressing inversions. But the nervous substance of Donne dictates his form, as in the figure of
the compasses:

> And though it in the centre sit,
>   Yet, when the other far doth roam,
> It leans, and hearkens after it,
>   And grows erect, as that comes home.

The evolution by which this form acquired the tune
of Marvell's stanza,

> My Love is of a birth as rare
> As 't is for object strange and high:
> It was begotten by despair
> Upon Impossibility,

probably must remain buried in the genius of the
age; but this fact cannot still the suspicion that Metaphysical content is intimately associated with Metaphysical form, and that where the *sense* is similar
the *sound* cannot be entirely different. The necessary
function of Jonson, it seems to me, was to teach the
Cavalier poets to get by art the dash which Donne
got by passionate intensity. Thus, where the feeling
was lighter, the thought had to be lightened; but the
paradoxical argument remained, and with it the rhetorical reinforcement of stress which created the
peculiar rise and fall of sound. This music was inherent in Donne's dialectic of passion.

From this general analysis of the fringe of the
Donne tradition, let us turn to the Cavalier poets
who were most responsive to the influence of Donne.

The two sides of this school could have no better illustration than the contrast between Herrick and Carew. They were poets of the same kind; each was characterized by the exquisite quality of his phrase and his numbers. They differed in their allegiance: one leaned as far toward Jonson as the other leaned toward Donne. We must put Suckling and Lovelace with Carew as the Cavalier poets most responsive to the influence of Donne, and therefore the best for illustrating the fringe of the Donne tradition.[1] One who could write an elegy for Donne in so thoroughly Donnean a fashion as Carew might be expected to show other marks of the Donne tradition. Nevertheless, we may well be amazed at the number of parallels with Donne that we find recorded in the notes to the edition of Carew published in *The Muses' Library*; and other parallels could be collected. All of Carew's best poems are Metaphysical: *Mediocrity in love rejected*, *To my inconstant Mistris*, *A deposition from love*, "*Ask me no more where Jove bestowes*," and *To a Lady that desired I would love her* are examples. Nor should we forget *Persuasions to Love*, the audacious but very Donnean *Rapture*, and the fine elegy to Donne. *Persuasions to Love* should be compared with Marvell's *Coy Mistress*: there is a similar progress from playful fancy to soaring passion on the theme of the Ausonian rose. While the conceits in this poem renew an old theme, something like a new

1. But even Herrick was touched by Donne, as *The Eye* indicates:
   Make me the straight, and oblique lines;
   The Motions, Lations, and the Signes. (Ed. Moorman, p. 47.)

prospect is opened on the emotion of love by the conceits in

> Now you have freely given me leave to love,
>   What will you doe?

In such poems the Metaphysical manner leads to real emotional discoveries, and betrays fresh intuitions of the heart.

In poems like *A deposition from love* we discover both the expanded conceit and the argument which knits the first line to the last. *To my inconstant Mistris* is Metaphysical in its conceit of excommunication, its tight logical structure, and its vehement close:

> When thou, poore excommunicate
>   From all the joyes of love, shalt see
> The full reward, and glorious fate,
>   Which my strong faith shall purchase me,
>   Then curse thine owne inconstancy.

Knowledge of Jonson was not sufficient to enable a man to write like this, though Jonson may have taught him to care for his phrasing and numbers. If we look at Carew's famous song in the "eights" quatrain, we shall see Jonson a little more in evidence:

> Ask me no more where *Jove* bestowes,
> When *June* is past, the fading rose:
> For in your beauties orient deep,
> These Flowers as in their causes sleep.

Only the last line betrays the unique marriage of concrete and abstract which characterizes Donne; the

rest of the song, however, contains other conceits of
the pretty sort of which Jonson was capable. The
last stanza is more Metaphysical, and offers a comparison that is illuminating:

> Ask me no more where those starres light,
> That downwards fall in dead of night:
> For in your eyes they sit, and there,
> Fixed, become as in their sphere.

Let us go back for a moment to Lord Herbert's *Ode*:

> This said, in her up-lifted face,
> Her eyes which did that beauty crown,
> Were like two starrs, that having faln down,
> Look up again to find their place.

The difference is apparent. Both are Metaphysical,
but Herbert's is more subtly and mysteriously so.
Jonson has intervened to make Carew's image less
difficult and more commonplace; it certainly is not
so beautiful as Herbert's, and it does not make so fine
a discovery of emotion. In these differences one can
see the influence of Jonson which draws Carew out to
the *fringe* of the Donne tradition. In *A Rapture*
Carew reflects the sensual side of Donne, and in
general he subscribes to the philosophy of love and
gallantry which Donne gave to the Cavalier school.

Unlike Carew, Sir John Suckling hardly represents
the serious side of Donne at all; but he raises the
levity of Donne to true "elfin laughter." His *"Why
so pale and wan, fond lover?"* is a legitimate development of the mockery latent in *Loves Exchange*. Likewise, his brusque opening of

> Out upon it! I have lov'd
> Three whole days together;

is in the tradition of "For Godsake hold your tongue, and let me love." When Suckling writes "Oh! for some honest Lovers ghost," recalling yet another first line of Donne, he shows us how far his talent was from the passionate intensity, as well as seriousness, of Donne. In this respect Carew came much closer to Donne, for even in sensuality Suckling is lighter than Carew.

Except for such a gay masterpiece as the *Ballad upon a Wedding*, Suckling's best poems belong to the fringe of the Donne tradition. Most of them are marked by some touch of the idea of variety in love, the cynical mockery, paradox, conceit, or argument found in this tradition. But the influence of Jonson is present in the general dilution of the Metaphysical qualities, in the clarity and concision of phrase, combined with the carelessness and ease of Suckling, as well as the rather commonplace thought. Although *Love's World* and the *Farewell to Love* give a burlesque effect to the Metaphysical manner, the conceit of love's siege,

> 'T is now, since I sat down before
> That foolish fort, a heart,

is a Suckling triumph in this style, sparkling with levity and wit. Other verses in the Metaphysical mode that deserve attention are the poems under *Sonnets*. But much of Suckling's work is marred by the slipshod faults of the careless amateur, the de-

fects peculiar to Cavalier poetry at its worst. One
cannot so truly say of the Cavaliers what Dr. Johnson
said of the Metaphysicals: "To write on their plan
it was at least necessary to read and think." That
discipline was becoming rather lax with them; hence
they could not afford to disregard Jonson's discipline
of art, but they did.

At least Suckling and Lovelace were guilty of such
neglect; Suckling wrote with the contemptuous scorn
of the improviser, and Lovelace with the carelessness
of the amateur and gentleman. Lovelace, however,
seems, more than Carew or Suckling, to have been
familiar with the classical lyrists; in fact, he made
numerous translations from Catullus, Martial, Auso-
nius, and others. Beginning with the Dedication to
Lucasta, Lovelace is obviously a follower of the ingenious Donne, though his own temperament is
quite seriously Petrarchian. Lovelace's imitation of
Donne is not only more extravagant, but also much
more solemn than that of Suckling. The bulk of his
verse is Metaphysical after the manner of Donne's
Flea, abounding in conceits such as those of *Ellinda's
Glove* or *Lucasta's Muff*, and now and then producing
conceits worse than the worst in Crashaw. In *A Loose
Saraband* love makes a whipping-top of his bleed-
ing heart; and in *Lucasta, Taking the Waters* he does
solemnly the sort of thing Donne does with savage
malice.

The fame of Lovelace rests upon two or three songs
which have the glory of expressing the ideal of the
Cavalier. These songs reveal the diluted Metaphysi-

cal quality which belongs to the fringe of the Donne tradition; in them the ingenuity of Lovelace has been tempered by emotion. Two of these songs are *Going to the Warres* and *To Althea from Prison*; a third is *Going beyond the Seas*, which is on the absence theme of *A Valediction: forbidding mourning*, and which is most memorable when it is most Metaphysical:

> Though Seas and Land be'twixt us both,
> > Our Faith and Troth,
> > Like separated soules,
> > All time and space controules:
> Above the highest sphere wee meet
> Unseene, unknowne, and greet as Angels greet.

While his two more famous songs have the conceits of a nunnery and a prison, this song has an astronomical figure, and *The Scrutinie* has Donne's theme of variety in love. Thus, all his best songs betray a happy relevance to the Donne tradition, though the bulk of his *Lucasta* is unflattering in its homage to Donne. *The Grasse-hopper* is a light Horatian ode of great charm, rather better in fancy than Cowley's poem on the same subject, but only Metaphysical in the fantastic touch about "green Ice" and "This *Aetna* in Epitome." Although we may conclude that we can well afford to spare Lovelace's extravagant imitation of Donne, we may reserve the feeling that this tradition lent an indefinable charm to the poems which came to suggest what 'Cavalier' meant when glorified by defeat.

The poets in the fringe of the Donne tradition, when they failed, failed because they neglected both the discipline in hard thinking and intense feeling of Donne and the discipline in conscious art of Jonson. Each discipline was in a way the corrective of the other, and each carried with it the possibilities of a definite kind of success; but neither was antithetical to the other in certain fundamental poetic ideals, and this accounts for the peculiar mixture of influence which made possible the variable but unified character of the Cavalier school. Herrick was most purely a son of Ben. In general the Cavaliers leaned in content toward Donne and in form toward Jonson; Donne was their genius, and Jonson their schoolmaster, and even he felt the persuasive force of Donne. We must remember that much of Donne's most characteristic love poetry was written before Jonson wrote his influential lyrics, and that Jonson was an open borrower of poetic wealth, while Donne was probably the most individual lyric poet that we have had in the whole range of English poetry.

But any discussion of the fringe of the Donne tradition — by no means exhausted by the Cavalier school — must deal largely with Jonson, who, after Donne, was the largest single influence on Caroline poetry. My examination of Jonson and the Cavalier school has led me to the conclusion that, even with Herrick outside, the main current of the Donne tradition embraces more talent and gives us a finer body of lyric verse than the Cavalier poets or any other group in the seventeenth century. This conclusion allows the sole exception of John Milton, and it does not forget the large and beneficial influence of

Jonson as a literary artist. The measure of Donne's tremendous and wayward influence is given by Jonson's own opinion that, although Donne should be hanged for not keeping accent, he was the first poet in the world in some things. It is to these things that we owe that corpus of Metaphysical poetry which, with all its shortcomings, is a treasure unlike any other in our language. The best justice that we can do its shortcomings is to judge them by the normal standards of good poetry, and not to excuse them in the name of quaintness and intellectual frippery. Let Jonson be such a standard, and we shall see two results: first, the Donne tradition will be established as no aberration, but as part of the English tradition of poetry, and in his own time as *the* tradition; and second, the Donne tradition will be found to contain a large body of verse that meets the usual requirements of English poetry, and at times as well as the finest.

Thus the fringe of this tradition, involving the powerful figure of Jonson, is of vital importance in placing the tradition in the current of English poetry. Because the current of poetry seems to have descended from Jonson to Dryden, we have been blinded to the fact that Donne and Jonson coöperated in moulding this current, which carried some of their qualities to the Augustans. In the next chapter we shall see why the discipline of Jonson prevailed over that of Donne, who was dominant in his own time. Meanwhile, it is sufficient to recognize that Donne connects with the past through Chapman, and with the future through Jonson.

IX. DRYDEN AND THE
REACTION

JOHN DRYDEN is important to any statement of the Donne tradition because we find in him the first sense of a Metaphysical school and of its definite conflict with a new tradition. His opinions are at once so flexible and precise that they become an excellent guide to the fate which the Donne tradition met in the latter part of the seventeenth century. His objections to Donne are valuable for a definition of Metaphysical poetry, while his growing reluctance to imitate Donne, who never quite lost his allegiance, shows how poetry changed with the Restoration and how Donne suffered by this change. Where Donne lost most was in the new conception of poetry to which Hobbes brought his genius for making definitions.

In 1651, just a year after the fifth edition of Donne's *Poems*, the text of the new esthetics appeared in the introductory essays to Sir William Davenant's *Gondibert*. With these essays Davenant and Hobbes, but chiefly Hobbes, set in motion the reaction which was to permit Donne's *Poems* but two more editions in the seventeenth century, the last coming in 1669. This count does not include an edition of the *Satires* in 1662 — a significant publication in this age. On the subject of poetic language — always of the great-

est importance to a poet — Hobbes reveals the changing poetic taste. First he objects to the current use
of words whose sound is greater than their sense, and
then continues,

> To this palpable darkness I may also add the ambitious
> obscurity of expressing more then is perfectly conceived, or
> perfect conception in fewer words then it requires. Which
> Expressions, though they have had the honor to be called
> strong lines, are indeed no better then Riddles, and, not
> onely to the Reader but also after a little time to the
> Writer himself, dark and troublesome.[1]

Some notion of the significance of this change of
taste may be got if we will recall what Chapman said
in his preface to *Ovid's Banquet of Sense*:

> Obscurity in affection of words and indigested conceits,
> is pedantical and childish; but where it shroudeth itself in
> the heart of his subject, uttered with fitness of figure and
> expressive epithets, with that darkness will I still labour
> to be shadowed. . . . I know that empty and dark spirits
> will complain of palpable night; but those that beforehand
> have a radiant and light-bearing intellect, will say they
> can pass through Corinna's garden without the help of a
> lantern.

Thus by 1651 Hobbes was complaining of palpable
night, and, like a literary Diogenes, crying for the
help of a lantern to pass through Corinna's garden.
With perfect adequacy of statement as the ideal of
poetry, it is easy to see what will happen to Donne.
Adequacy will triumph till we have the language of
Dryden, whose denotation is immense but whose
suggestiveness is almost nothing.

1. Spingarn, *Critical Essays of the Seventeenth Century*, ii, 63.

The blow, however, that was to prove fatal to Donne's reputation as a poet was Hobbes's dissection of the imagination:

Time and Education begets experience; Experience begets memory; Memory begets Judgement and Fancy; Judgement begets the strength and structure, and Fancy begets the ornaments of a Poem.[1]

Thus imagination is no longer central and vital in the poetic process, but merely an adjunct to it, for Hobbes ignores the transforming power of the imagination for the sake of the recording power. In his *Leviathan* he makes his famous distinction between wit and judgment, which Professor Spingarn summarizes in these words:

'wit,' the current term for fancy, denotes quickness of mind in seeing the resemblances between disparate objects; judgement, or reason, finds differences in objects apparently similar.[2]

Hobbes concludes that "Judgment therefore without fancy is wit, but fancy without judgment, not." In Hobbes the supremacy of judgment is already patent; and it was to increase in authority until Dryden could define wit as "a propriety of thoughts and words," in which the element of fancy is entirely lost. When we remember that for Donne wit was a kind of intellectual imaginativeness, we can see how far we have come. With such a revolution in esthetics

1. Spingarn, *op. cit.*, ii, 59.
2. *Ibid.*, i, xxix. See *Leviathan*, i, 8.

it is not surprising that imagination came to be regarded as little more than a frisky faculty, and even by Hobbes as "decaying sense." [1]

Before judgment became the great arbiter of poetry, Donne was still admired for his wit, though in the sense of the quick perception of similarity in difference; that is, ingenuity. For Donne was witty in this sense also. But when the new esthetics had come to dominate poetry, Donne, when he was remembered, could only be remembered for what suffered least by this change of taste — his satire. Only when men revised their idea of the imagination could Donne recover a genuine hold upon the interests of readers, and that time did not come till Wordsworth and Coleridge. This is not to say, however, that Donne did not continue to exert an influence upon Dryden. Finally, this new conception of poetry explains why Donne's influence upon Cleveland took the form it did: the two traditions of poetry were at odds, and Cleveland stood between them, paying allegiance to Donne with the sensibility of the new age.

Now let us see how this change of taste serves to define the Donne tradition. Dryden shall be our guide. Although he has a good deal to say about Donne and Cowley in the course of his career, he says the most significant things in the last decade of the century. Having felt some resemblance between Donne and Cleveland as early as his *Essay of Dramatic Poesy,* in which he compares Cleveland's satires very unfavorably with Donne's, he definitely yokes

---

1 See *Leviathan*, i, 2 (ed. Routledge and Sons, pp. 3–4).

Cowley with Donne as a writer who "affects the metaphysics" when he pens his *Original and Progress of Satire* in 1692. These are the only Metaphysical poets whom Dryden ever mentions, unless Quarles be counted as such; and yet in this essay Dryden unwittingly became the christener of this school and the source of our chief notion of its character. Discounting the incense which he burns for Dorset, let us look at this important passage:

> Donne alone, of all our countrymen, had your talent; but was not happy enough to arrive at your versification; and were he translated into numbers, and English, he would yet be wanting in the dignity of expression. . . . You equal Donne in the variety, multiplicity, and choice of thoughts; you excel him in the manner and the words. I read you both with the same admiration, but not with the same delight. He affects the metaphysics, not only in his satires, but in his amorous verses, where nature only should reign.[1]

A year before, Dryden had called Donne "the greatest Wit, though not the best Poet, of our Nation."[2] Now he adds, "I may safely say it of this present age, that if we are not so great wits as Donne, yet certainly we are better poets."[3] This passage is very illuminating: its conclusion is what we should expect from the new esthetics, but it cannot conceal its admiration of Donne. It also begins the alienation of Donne from the main tradition of English poetry

---

1. W. P. Ker, *Essays of John Dryden*, ii, 19.
2. See Dedication of *Eleonora*, Sargeaunt, *Dryden's Poetical Works*, p. 185.
3. W. P. Ker, *op. cit.*, ii, 102.

when it suggests his translation into numbers and English.

In 1700, when the new ideas of imagination, nature, wit, and versification had become established, Dryden wrote the passage which definitely outmoded the Metaphysical poets. It is in the *Preface to the Fables*. He doubtless had Cowley in mind, but since Cowley was the last Metaphysical to go out of style, we are justified in regarding the criticism as a blanket judgment of the whole school, which Dryden only vaguely realized as a school.

> One of our late great poets is sunk in his reputation, because he could never forgive any conceit which came in his way; but swept like a drag-net, great and small . . . . All this proceeded not from any want of knowledge, but of judgment. Neither did he want that in discerning the beauties and faults of other poets, but only indulged himself in the luxury of writing; and perhaps knew it was a fault, but hoped the reader would not find it. For this reason, though he must always be thought a great poet, he is no longer esteemed a good writer; and for ten impressions, which his works have had in so many successive years, yet at present a hundred books are scarcely purchased once a twelve-month.[1]

And we must remember that from the Restoration to the age of Pope, Cowley was reprinted oftener than any other Metaphysical poet. With the passing of the Metaphysicals, we witness the triumph of the "good writer" and the Neo-classical view of literature.

But the influence of the Metaphysical tradition on Dryden never entirely passed away. Dryden, as Van

1. *Ibid.*, p. 258.

Doren has said in his fine study, "was never exempt from conceits as long as he lived." [1] In fact, the conceit may be said to survive in Augustan poetry in the circumlocution, which is nearer the *préciosité* that Molière satirizes than it is to the Metaphysical conceit, which is commonly regarded as the English counterpart of the European phenomenon. While the darling of his youth, the famous Cowley, — as Dryden called him in 1693, — was generally the model for conceits such as those in the poem on Lord Hastings or scientific figures such as those in the *Heroic Stanzas*, it is to Donne that they must finally be traced. Mr. Van Doren attributes the nature of the images, such as the image of circles, in these poems and in *Astraea Redux*, *The Hind and the Panther*, and *Eleonora*, to the influence of scholasticism; [2] but this neglects the fact that Donne had taught English poets to use scholasticism in poetry, and it neglects the influence of Donne in these poems — by Dryden's own word, in the *Eleonora*. This poem by Dryden in the last decade of his life has among its prefatory words this tribute:

Doctor Donn the greatest Wit, though not the best Poet, of our Nation, acknowledges that he had never seen Mrs. Drury, whom he has made immortal in his admirable *Anniversaries*; I have had the same fortune; though I have not succeeded to the same Genius. However, I have followed his footsteps in the Design of his Panegyrick.

Turning back a few years to the *Ode to Mrs. Anne*

1. Mark Van Doren, *The Poetry of John Dryden*, p. 24.
2. *Ibid.*, p. 16.

Killigrew, we may hear Donne's voice, though with a Neo-classical accent, in such lines as

> And there the last *Assizes* keep
> For those who Wake and those who Sleep;
> When ratling *Bones* together fly
> From the four Corners of the Skie,[1]

and we may remember, with pleasant malice, that this ode derives its present esteem from Dr. Johnson.

Although Dryden declared against the conceit from the first, he was not so rigorous in his practice but that he succumbed to the lure of Donne's image and even courted the scientific figure that Donne had found "a brighter ornament for verse than hackneyed mythology."[2] While we may agree with Van Doren that Dryden established what Macaulay called "the scientific vocabulary" in verse,[3] we must not forget that Donne was before him in this field, and that this innovation was one of the main items that distinguished Donne for a man like Carew. In fact, one of the things which must strike us more and more as we study the Donne tradition is the fertilizing influence that Donne has had on the imagery of English verse.

But this was not all that Dryden could claim as the heir of the passing tradition, for there he could learn "the secret architecture of reasoned verse," which

1. Compare *Holy Sonnet* vii:
>   At the round earths imagin'd corners, blow
>   Your trumpets, Angells, and arise, arise
>   From death, you numberlesse infinities
>   Of soules, and to your scattred bodies goe.
2. See the conceits listed in Johnson's *Life of Dryden*.
3. Van Doren, *op. cit.*, p. 18.

Van Doren says he learned from Lucretius.[1] However, one is readier to believe that Van Doren has hit upon the secret of this architecture when he relates Dryden's way of thinking to the scholastic forms which Dryden met at Cambridge.[2] But English verse had already learned at the hands of Donne to follow the involutions of scholastic reasoning; and it is more probable that a young poet would learn this from one who had already fascinated his youthful imagination than it is that he would strike out for himself, or learn scholastic architecture from a Latin poet. Certain censures of the eighteenth century confirm us in this belief. Swift called *The Hind and the Panther* "a complete abstract of sixteen thousand schoolmen, from Scotus to Bellarmine"; and Cowper, in the *Task*, rebuked Cowley with these words:

> I cannot but lament thy splendid wit
> Entangled in the cobwebs of the schools.[3]

Such censures carry us inevitably back to Donne, whose example seduced minds which were not naturally scholastic, but which were already pregnant with the attitude that was to produce these censures.

Whether we grant that the ratiocinative quality in Dryden came from Donne or not, we must admit that the ratiocinative processes are a distinguishing mark of Donne's verse and that Dryden was aware of this, for he charges Donne with affecting the metaphysics. Indeed it might be said that ratiocination

1. Van Doren, *op. cit.*, p. 12.
2. *Ibid.*, p. 16.
3. *Ibid.*

was what the new tradition did not reject, but that, tempered to the new taste, ratiocination became a characteristic quality of Neo-classical poetry.   If Dryden charges that Donne "perplexes the minds of the fair sex with nice speculations of philosophy, when he should ingage their hearts, and entertain them with the softnesses of love," he also realizes that "it requires Philosophy, as well as Poetry, to sound the depth of all the passions."[1] And Dryden was enamored of this philosophy all his life long, though he never won it, except in the ratiocinative ordering of his thoughts.

The qualities of Donne which may be said to earn the suffrage and imitation of the Neo-classical tradition appear in their most congenial form in his satires and poetic epistles. It is in connection with his satires that his reputation as a wit seems to have survived. This is not surprising, for Donne was, if not the first, very nearly the first writer of classical satire in English, and this was the favorite form of the Augustans. The wit and matter of his satires were not uncongenial to the new taste which Hobbes had formulated in his definition of wit and in his assertion that the "manners of men" are the proper subject of poetry.[2] In fact Donne, in his first satire, had drawn the first portrait of the Sir Fopling Flutter who was to adorn so many pages of Restoration literature. And many of Donne's witty satirical images were not to be lost to the Augustans while Pope's memory lasted; nor

1. Ker, *op. cit.*, ii, 19.
2. Spingarn, *op. cit.*, ii, 56.

was "the greatest Wit, though not the best Poet, of our Nation" to be forgotten while Dryden kept his voice.

If Dryden's youth thus reveals the influence of Donne, and if that influence never quite died out in him, it was Jonson's discipline of conscious art that became the master of Dryden's maturity. This discipline was in harmony with the Neo-classical influence which came from France at this time and earned the rather Jesuitical suffrage of Dryden. Furthermore, the structure of the Restoration sensibility required such a discipline of reason, order, and conscious art, as we have seen in its new esthetics. Hence, the reasons for the depression of Donne were just those which guaranteed the rise of Jonson: the qualities in which Donne differed from Jonson were going out of style, and were to remain out of favor as long as classicism kept its hold on English literature. This change in the structure of the English sensibility is all that prevented the current of poetry from descending in a direct line from the Metaphysicals, as it had descended in a direct line to them. Even so late as the Restoration the influence of Donne was irresistible to many poets, but no influence was powerful enough to controvert a sensibility that revised Shakspere. The times were favorable to Jonson, with certain reservations. Almost the whole truth is that the Elizabethan age descended to the Restoration through Jonson.

It is to the honor of Dryden that in the reaction against things Elizabethan he was capable of generous appreciation as well as the strictures of his age. Although he alone seems to have been conscious of the full antagonism of his age to Donne, he neglects neither to praise Donne nor to imitate him. It is a very significant fact that the two great critics of the seventeenth century, Jonson and Dryden, never object to Donne's conceits, though Dryden did censure Cowley and Cleveland for theirs. And yet the conceit has been the chief criticism of the Metaphysicals since the age of Pope, and especially since Dr. Johnson. What Dryden actually says of Donne's wit and conceit makes a very instructive comparison with Dr. Johnson's criticism. Dryden thus concludes a discussion of Clevelandisms:

but we cannot read a verse of Cleveland's without making a face at it, as if every word were a pill to swallow: he gives us many times a hard nut to break our teeth, without a kernel for our pains. So that there is this difference betwixt his *Satires* and doctor Donne's; that the one gives us deep thoughts in common language, though rough cadence; the other gives us common thoughts in abstruse words: 'tis true, in some places his wit is independent of his words, as in that of the *Rebel Scot*:

> Had *Cain* been *Scot*, God would have chang'd his doom;
> Not forc'd him wander, but confined him home.

Si sic omnia dixisset! This is wit in all languages: 'tis like Mercury, never to be lost or killed: — and so that other —

> For beauty, like white powder, makes no noise,
> And yet the silent hypocrite destroys.

You see, the last line is highly metaphorical, but it is so soft and gentle, that it does not shock us as we read it.[1]

It is easy to see that here we have the germ of Dr. Johnson's notion of Metaphysical wit, but Dryden is friendly to Donne and much more fair. His last quotation from Cleveland would certainly be pronounced to be a conceit, and yet to Dryden it is but highly metaphorical, and not displeasing so long as it does not shock the mind into rejection. Here Dryden is judging the figure by the normal standards of poetry; he does not put even the Clevelandism down as a monstrosity, but judges it by the standards of Ovid and Virgil. Donne is exonerated for the sake of his "deep thoughts." The first quotation from Cleveland represents the balanced sort of wit which Dryden was to perfect, but Dryden judges it by the same standard that he applied to the distinctly Metaphysical sort. If Dr. Johnson had followed Dryden in this respect, we should today have a much fairer view of the Donne tradition. Although this criticism represents the opinion of Dryden in 1668, being from the *Essay of Dramatic Poesy*, it was never explicitly controverted by his later criticism. Even in his censure of Cowley in 1700 he does not object so much to the conceit as to Cowley's want of selection.

But the age of Dryden undoubtedly felt that it had learned certain things about the use of images and words that made it superior to its predecessors. This feeling colors Dryden's criticism of Shakspere,

1. Ker, *op. cit.*, i, 52–53.

and comes out explicitly in his definition of wit and the "turn." Judgment, as both Hobbes and Dryden inform us, is the supreme arbiter in these matters: "Judgment therefore without fancy is wit, but fancy without judgment, not."

One may account for this evolution in the use of the image from the time of Elizabeth by the following theory. The Elizabethan conceit as used by Sir Philip Sidney was essentially decorative, primarily suggestive in its function, designed to throw a nebula of pretty light over its object. The Metaphysical conceit adventured in a new direction: it refused nothing in its intense desire for expression; it sought whatever would make its feeling precise, whatever would interpret reality and the darkest recesses of the mind. Being intent upon exact and compelling expression, it became careless of the suggestive power of words in its eagerness to state the new conquest of learning and experience, of the subtleties of mind and heart. When these motives disappeared, the language became hollow and merely ingenious; with the deep thoughts gone, the images were simply reprehensible. Since these images had been peculiarly scientific and primarily denotative in purpose, their suggestions became shocking or ludicrous when their thoughtfulness disappeared. Finally, in Dryden the denotative tendency persists, with the added impulse to suppress suggestiveness or *magic* altogether. In short, the theory is that imagination is supreme in the Elizabethan image, that imagination and reason are contending in the Metaphysical image, and that reason is supreme in the Neo-classical image. For support in his poetics Dryden could look back to Jonson and classical reason.

When this reaction to the Donne tradition had attained consciousness in Dryden, the separation of the high style of the Elizabethans into wit and magniloquence was complete. This separation we first saw distinctly in Cowley; now it gives us *Mac Flecknoe* and *The Conquest of Granada*, and terminates the dissociation of Jonson's "rhetoric." In these works we become aware of a new sensibility and of a new structure of art which serve to define Metaphysical poetry. When Dryden pays tribute to the conscious art of Jonson in the elegy to Oldham, we perceive that the current of poetry no longer descends from the Donne tradition, or from the elegies in which Jonson imitated Donne, but rather from the *Elegy on Lady Jane Pawlet*.

X. A SHORT VIEW OF THE TRADITION

>>◇◇<<

O UR CRITICAL view of the Donne tradition is obscured by the imposing shadow of Dr. Johnson. His classification of the so-called Metaphysical poets has colored all later criticism, although his canons of taste — strong as they are within their own limits — have long been out of style. The reputation of the Metaphysical poets, which Professor Nethercot has traced for us, shows how dependent Dr. Johnson was upon the neo-classical critics who preceded him; nevertheless, Dr. Johnson is responsible for the view of the Donne tradition which literary history reflects today. In that view I detect certain false lights and a rather strained perspective. It is time that these were corrected.

Dr. Johnson's criticism begins with this statement:

About the beginning of the seventeenth century appeared a race of writers that may be termed the metaphysical poets; of whom, in a criticism of the works of Cowley, it is not improper to give some account.[1]

It is doubtless too late to change the name "metaphysical," but that has not prevented several critics from exclaiming against its lack of propriety. While recognizing the futility of such complaint at this

---

1. See his *Life of Cowley*.

late day, I have preferred to group these poets as representative of the Donne tradition, much as one might speak of the Dryden tradition. After all, affecting the metaphysics is a perilous trait by which to distinguish a group of writers of English poetry.

A more serious question is to what extent these poets may be said to have formed a school. Professor Nethercot's study of their reputation shows conclusively that they did not form a school for their contemporaries, and only very vaguely for Dryden. Pope was the first to formulate a school of Donne; his list was first printed in Ruffhead's *Life* in 1769.[1] It included a strange assortment: Cowley, Davenant, Michael Drayton, Sir Thomas Overbury, Randolph, Sir John Davis, Sir John Beaumont, Cartwright, Cleveland, Crashaw, Bishop Corbet, Lord Falkland, Carew, T. Carey, G. Sandys, Fairfax, Sir John Mennis, and Tho. Baynal. To Pope, who was wider read in these poets than Dryden and farther removed from them, this was the school of Donne. In this list we find several poets who were sealed of the tribe of Ben. Later, Dr. Johnson adds to the confusion when he speaks of Ben Jonson as one whose example recommended Metaphysical writing. The significant thing is that, even for poets, the school of Donne is very hard to limit in the current of seventeenth-century poetry. The fact is that there was no sealed tribe of Donne, though his influence was the

1. This list is cited by Nethercot in "The Reputation of the 'Metaphysical Poets' during the Age of Pope," *Philological Quarterly*, vol. iv, no. 2, p. 170.

most profound and pervasive of any in the first half
of his century.

Our study of the poets themselves bears out this
conclusion. And this study may be related to certain
facts regarding the age itself. One is the remarkable
ease with which the authorship of poems could be
confused. We have seen how in the case of Jonson
and Donne, the two great influences of the age, it was
possible for the work of one to be ascribed to the
other. The difficulty of determining the canon of
these seventeenth-century poets is eloquent of this
fact, even for so individual a genius as Donne. The
absence of any sharply defined school of Donne is
also attested by the number of poets in *Jonsonus
Virbius* who not only saluted Donne with resounding
elegies but also imitated him. Furthermore, the difficulty with which Dryden, Pope, and later critics
have determined just what poets are to be termed
"metaphysical" indicates the uncertain limits of such
a school, and the real profundity of Donne's influence.

This influence may be called the Donne tradition,
but it cannot be detached from the common sensibility of the age and regarded as outside the structure
of art peculiar to that sensibility. With these limita-
tions the tradition may be called a "movement," but
a movement which must be defined in the wise words
of M. André Gide: "Influence creates nothing; it
awakens something." Hence this tradition is a movement to the extent that Donne's influence, generally
pervasive, awakened more in some poets than in

others; such poets belong to his tradition. With this principle of selection, I have therefore chosen for this tradition the poets who, after careful study, seemed to me to come nearest to Donne. This study became more difficult when I realized that he was in harmony with his age and not fundamentally antithetical to Jonson, whose influence even coöperates in certain directions with that of Donne. For Donne, the supreme influence, was yet a product of his age, and must be related to the structure of art founded upon the general sensibility of that age.

If we look at the structure of art which this age produced, we shall be able to orient the Donne tradition with greater justice. Perhaps nothing is more striking than the erudite temper of the Jacobeans; it has added an abundant store of learning to literature: of classical learning in such men as Chapman and Jonson; of strange lore and mixed learning in men like Burton and Donne. Then there is the new science and mighty sweep of thought in Bacon; and later the quaint learning and curious beauty of Sir Thomas Browne, who gives us perhaps our best hint of the place of the fantastic in this literature. Not far away is Florio's translation of Bacon's model in the essay — Montaigne, whose subtle and inquisitive mind colored the work of Bacon, Webster, Marston, Shakspere, and no doubt much of the Jacobean temper. Certainly, among all the ingredients of this sensibility, the scepticism of Montaigne was no small item, for Mr. Charles Crawford has uncovered the large debt to Montaigne of dramatists like

Webster and Marston.[1] Moreover, the drift toward complexity of thought and subtlety of feeling may be seen in the so-called decadent tone of Jacobean drama, with its pursuit of strange emotion.

The Jacobean sensibility finds characteristic expression in the *Anatomy of Melancholy* and *Urn Burial*, as well as in the Jacobean drama; for all indulge in the new subtleties of feeling and thought.[2] In Mr. Crawford's study we find further evidence to show that the Jacobean sensibility was pervasive and not confined to any water-tight compartments, that it flowed freely from prose to play, and from play to poem. For *The Duchess of Malfi* Webster borrows material from the poems of Chapman and Donne, as well as from Sidney, Jonson, Montaigne, and Bacon. Frequently Webster uses the same borrowings in his play, *The Duchess of Malfi*, and his poem, *A Monumental Column*; especially is this true of his borrowings from Donne. The sensibility of Webster found little difficulty in harmonizing such loans, since most of them were marked by the familiar stamp of the age. I have already indicated how a dramatist like Chapman was related to the style of poetry we find in Donne. It is disastrous to neglect the fact that the same sensibility was producing parallel results in the lyric and dramatic verse of this age. We could ask

1. See *Collectanea, Second Series*: "Montaigne, Webster, and Marston: Donne and Webster." On Donne's relation to scepticism see L. I. Bredvold's "Religious Thought of Donne," *Studies in Shakespeare, Milton, and Donne*.

2. The Jacobean sensibility persists throughout the first half of the century.

for no more concrete example of the unity of this sensibility than the liberal debt of the *Duchess of Malfi* to the *Anniversaries* of Donne, were we not already aware of the sameness of mood in both poets. As late as John Hall this sensibility had almost the power of magic; such power explains Professor Saintsbury's remark that Hall "has the poetic measles itself as clearly as ever man had." [1]

Nor can we neglect this sensibility as it appears in the great preachers of the time. There is Richard Hooker with his two themes of revelation and reason, but eminent in ratiocination and constructive powers which owe much to St. Thomas Aquinas, and controlled by the rationalism, rather than the mysticism, which flowed through the seventeenth century. More popular and more typical, however, are Bishop Andrewes and Doctor Donne. Andrewes, with his immense learning, famous wit, and fanciful rhetoric, gave way to the macabre imagination and blazing intensity of Donne when he turned his extraordinary abilities to the pulpit. The qualities which have been termed "metaphysical" commanded the highest places in the Church of that age. Even the Bible of 1611, translated under the supervision of Bishop Andrewes, reflects the sensibility of the age in its troubled obscurity and its bold and homely metaphorical language. In fact, the mysticism and so-called quaintness of the Metaphysical poets have vital kinship with our

1. *Caroline Poets*, ii, 178. Even Sir Thomas Browne's earliest published work was a Donnean elegy to Donne. See Grierson, *Donne's Poetical Works*, i, 372.

finest translation of the Bible, for that kinship is strangely evident in the fantastic excesses of such a poet as Edward Benlowes.

In this age of notably erudite men, we should expect to find their erudition incorporated into their poetry, once we had felt the power of their sensibility. We are, nevertheless, surprised at the vigor of this incorporation in Donne, and only less so at that in Chapman and Jonson. Our surprise is explained when we notice that this incorporation of learning has the emphasis of a conscious revolution in poetry. Some words in Jonson's *Conversations with Drummond* indicate the direction of this revolt: "That verses stood by sense without colours or accent; *which yett other tymes he denied.*" [1] This preference of *meaning* to *ornament* or *sound* was certainly shared by Donne. But Chapman, as his preface to *Ovid's Banquet of Sense* shows, also belongs with Jonson and Donne in this intellectual revolt in poetry; all three sought to enlarge the intellectual compass of poetry and to develop a masculine and astringent verse, charged with thought and expressed with unaffected and vital directness of language. Their images were not embroidery, but the necessary structure of their feeling and thought. Chapman, Jonson, and Donne were notably men who incorporated their reading into their poetry, who derived poetic inspiration from learning. In view of the sensibility of this age, the conclusion is plain: these men added the conscious impetus of determined minds to the inclination of the age.

1. Cunningham, *Works of Ben Jonson*, vol. iii, p. 486, sec. xv.

We now have before us a brief sketch of the sensibility of this age and of the structure of art which it created. The question which next arises is how far the Donne tradition may be said to be a digression from the main current of poetry. Jacobean literature has already appeared to us as a development of Elizabethan literature in a new direction. Donne simply adds the force of genius to this bent; in no other sense can his tradition be called a digression. Behind all his amazing originality there is the inclination of his age, as well as a poetic revolution abetted by Chapman and Jonson. The support which his time lent to his genius accounts for the tremendous vitality of his influence and its strange capacity for touching the most diverse talent. It is profoundly true that Donne created nothing in his disciples, but he awakened something. He awakened them to the spirit of the age and to their own peculiar embodiment of it.

In general the influence of Donne upon the bent of Jacobean poetry may be characterized as one of emphasis. He went further in certain directions than Chapman and Jonson; in other directions he added possibilities that they either neglected or did not see. The force of genius carried him more vigorously against the facile and easy in rhythm and music, and more powerfully towards original and fresh imagery, towards almost colloquial directness of language, towards the intellectual evolution of the poem, towards wit as part of the texture of poetry, and towards the necessity of wide interests for the poet. In all of these directions his genius augmented the inclination of the age. In these directions his disciples approach him, though perhaps least in the masculine expression which lacks the tuned chime; and yet if they recover the melody, they do not forget to trouble it with thought. But of course Donne himself does not lack a haunting though hardy music that is born of intense emotion.

However, Donne's closest disciples are awakened in a profounder way by what we may call the trinity of his genius, his mysticism, logic, and passionate intensity. These are the qualities which made his thinking and feeling individual in his own age; these are signs by which we recognize the poets who belong to the Donne tradition. We should not forget, however, that two powerful currents of thought, one mystical and the other rationalistic, flowed through the seventeenth century and reinforced Donne's mysticism and logic; only in his peculiar intensity and in his indefinable combination of all three qualities was he unique and incomparable.[1]

Such a view of Donne in relation to his age requires us to make some qualification of Professor Courthope's account of poetical "Wit." In my analysis of the Donne tradition, I have suggested the modification that seems necessary for what Courthope calls "the leading features of 'Wit,' namely (1) Paradox, (2) Hyperbole, (3) Excess of Metaphor."[2] The origin of this "Wit" Courthope traces to

[1] Donne's relation to the currents of thought in his age is discussed in the admirable studies of Prof. L. I. Bredvold which I cite in Appendix D.

2. *History of English Poetry*, iii, 106.

the crumbling of the medieval system of thought in collision with the forces of the Renascence, and concludes that since all of these qualities of "Wit" appear in the older system of thought, "their predominance in the later age signifies the efflorescence of decay." [1] In other words, he seems to agree with Remy de Gourmont that "the idea of decadence is identical with the idea of imitation." [2] But Courthope might not agree with Gourmont that this idea of literary decadence derives from the simple idea of absence, the lack of superior intelligences and the dominance of imitative mediocrity. Strictly speaking, Donne cannot be brought under this very just description of literary decadence, which is implicit in Courthope's condemnation. On the other hand, Dr. Johnson, while objecting to Donne, assimilated the idea of decadence to its exact opposite — the idea of innovation. In the face of such confusion it seems to me that we must declare that poetry which corresponds so closely as Metaphysical poetry does to the general sensibility of its age cannot in strict truth be called "the efflorescence of decay." For the Metaphysical poets were not so imitative as the Elizabethan poets, and they certainly produced vigorous and novel blossoms with vital roots in sincerity. For that matter, scholastic reasoning has even left its mark on so late and different a poet as Dryden.

And surely we have never had an art structure so adapted to mystical expression as that which these

1. *Op. cit.*, chap. vi, "Nature and Origin of Poetical 'Wit.'"
2. See *Decadence* (trans. W. A. Bradley), p. 145.

poets created upon the basis of their sensibility! Professor Courthope excuses Dante's enigmatic and abundant imagery on the ground that it was the logical and necessary consequence of his subject-matter, because Dante was describing the nature of the unseen world and only by such imagery could he make the reality of his experience clear.[1] But so were the Metaphysicals, in their smaller way, describing the nature of the unseen world of life, love, death, and eternity. What else was Donne doing "at the round earths imagin'd corners"? or Vaughan when he "saw Eternity the other night"? or Marvell when he heard "Times winged Charriot hurrying near"? or even Lovelace when he told Lucasta,

> Above the highest sphere wee meet,
> Unseene, unknowne, and greet as angels greet?

The plain truth is that where poetry conquers, it is useless to speak of so-called vices like paradox, hyperbole, excess of metaphor, and the efflorescence of decay; or to call them the crying defects of a certain kind of poetry.[2] Only when poetry fails do we become conscious of the defects of its qualities, or when a change of taste makes us abnormally sensitive to the things we lack or deplore. We shall do the Donne tradition greater justice if we cease to judge it by defects, or like it for them, and judge it instead by the normal standards of poetry. Then we shall not be forever speaking of it as "metaphysical" or

1. See *op. cit.*, pp. 110–112.
2. Donne's vice is "not the daring of adventure but of intensity."

"witty," "quaint" or "obscure," but rather at its best as no more to be estimated by these qualities than other serious poetry. By such an approach we shall not formulate lists of capital virtues and defects which the first breath of poetry may throw into confusion.

It is nevertheless true that the Donne tradition has emphasized certain qualities which we find in poetry, and has therefore earned its peculiar reputation. These qualities I have enumerated in my discussion of how far this tradition might be regarded as a digression from the main current; their emphasis was, as we saw, to be explained by the genius of Donne. Any influence must, I suppose, be regarded as one of mingled good and bad; almost never can one be called wholly good or bad. If I have made the nature of Metaphysical poetry clear, I have shown that its defects are, in a very true sense, the defects of its qualities, and that as such they have earned abundant criticism. We may now proceed to a rather neglected but more interesting question. What do we owe to the Donne tradition as an inheritance of genuine poetic value?

Dr. Johnson answered that we owe some verse to it, but no poetry. Of course this answer can no longer be accepted. But we do agree with him that the Metaphysical poets were men of learning, original, analytic, and subtle, though we cannot agree that they could not move the affections. To his other charges, we may answer that if they lacked sublimity, they had a very good substitute; that it is sometimes desirable for poets to depart from nature as he understood it; and that elegance and "high" diction are not the sole criteria for language. But this is only to say that we know that Metaphysical poetry cannot answer to the standards of the neo-classical tradition. It does, however, answer to the broader standards of poetry as a form of art.

In actual poetry we owe to the Donne tradition more than we have been willing to admit, more than appears in our anthologies, and more in influence than any age since Dryden. In devotional poetry no other age in English verse has equalled this tradition. I might have said "religious" poetry, but I prefer to use T. S. Eliot's distinction: "Devotional poetry is religious poetry which falls within an exact faith and has precise objects for contemplation." [1] Although Herbert is not a mystic in the sense in which Crashaw and Vaughan are mystics, he wrote the purest devotional poetry in the seventeenth century. Of devotional poetry which conveys genuine mystical experience, Crashaw produces the most ecstatic examples, Vaughan reveals flashes of the rarest sort, and Benlowes presents the most fantastic form in this century. When we add to this religious verse the intense presence of Donne's supernatural passion, we have a body of devotional poetry unsurpassed in the language. The peculiar difficulty of religious poetry — witnessed by our dearth of it — makes this conclusion a token of great worth.

1. "The Poetry of Richard Crashaw," *The Dial*, vol. lxxxiv, no. 3, p. 250.

In love poetry the Donne tradition is only less radiant, not less individual. The curious exploration of the soul — so marked a trait in these poets — added a new range to the language of the heart in the love lyrics of Donne. Neither our psychology nor our philosophy of love has been the same since Donne; the difference is the difference between Browning and Sir Philip Sidney, and is also manifest in such poets as Meredith and Rupert Brooke. In this knowledge neither Jonson nor Milton, but only Donne in the seventeenth century, went beyond the point where Shakspere left off. And none of the followers of Donne had his power over the heart, but all learned from him some of the magic which carries the heart into the disturbance of the mind and beyond the reaches of the soul. Lord Herbert, King, Marvell, and Townshend achieved fine things in the Metaphysical language of the heart, and most of the Cavaliers captured something of this Metaphysical overtone, which touches much that is neither devotional nor love poetry in this age. The music of the Metaphysicals, though seldom as rugged as Donne's, is primarily a music of ideas like his. At its highest the Caroline cadence is as haunting as this poetry is arresting in imagery; this cadence has not, I think, been over-praised by Professor Saintsbury, who says that nobody had it before and nobody has got it since, except by imitation.[1] The most magnificent instance of this cadence is probably to be found in Marvell's *Definition of Love*.

1. *Op. cit.*, vol. i, p. viii.

Somewhere we should include Cleveland's witty and satiric achievements in this tradition, as well as Cowley's use of it in his fine poems of levity and analysis. And scattered among the Metaphysicals there are also memorable things in eulogy and elegy that are a tribute to the Donne tradition and a treasure for English poetry. All in all, this tradition not only belongs to the main current of poetry, but invites our appreciation to verse as fine of its kind as any in our language. In spite of frequent lapses and perhaps less constant art, the Donne tradition is more interesting and greater in richness and variety of experience than Cavalier poetry. In fact, it has produced the finest body of arresting lyric poetry in the seventeenth century, and of particular kinds unmatched in any later time.

Besides giving us this body of fine poetry, the Donne tradition has been an unmeasured force in the development of poetry. In an essay on *The Progress of Poetry* Mr. F. L. Lucas makes this statement:

It is in fact towards more brain that poetry must probably continue to travel, as it has travelled since it began. There is no going back. If the reason has taken much, it has given other things; if it destroyed the ballad, it brought us Donne; we need more of it, not less.[1]

We may choose to dispute this prediction, but we can hardly doubt the remark concerning Donne. Certainly he brought more brain work into poetry and stamped an age that was friendly to thinking. There

1. *Authors Dead and Living*, p. 294.

is no more striking trait of the Metaphysical lyric than the brain work evident in its images and structure. As opposed to the simple, sensuous, and passionate tradition, Donne is complex, sensuous, and intellectual. The critics who call his method one of abstraction, and point to *The Extasie*, are surely victims of confusion: Donne often deals in abstractions, but he usually puts them concretely; witness *The Extasie*. Even when he illustrates sensuous experience by means of abstractions, he produces such a blend of sense and thought as no mere abstraction could ever have.

In passing from the Elizabethan lyric to the lyric of Donne, we encounter a question that may have provoked Milton's definition of poetry, but which still troubles us today. How far is the poetic faculty compatible with the other activities of the mind? Despite Milton's definition — not then written of course — Donne's tremendous intensity succeeded in blending ratiocinative processes with the poetic process, and thus in producing remarkable poetry. In this, as in other ways, such as the possible interests of the poet, he extended the bounds of poetry, although we have not proved very willing to accept this extension. And thus Donne's influence on poetry has been in the direction of more brain, with the consequent tendency to stress meaning rather than music.

This emphasis of brain work in poetry produced in Donne a kind of imagery that has had untold consequences for English verse. His imagery can in fact be regarded as an early adventure into the field since exploited by the Symbolists. This imagery, which has become famous for its faults, may yet have lessons for the future of intellectual poetry, as it has had for the past. It is difficult not to see in the images of Browning, Rossetti, Meredith, Coventry Patmore, Francis Thompson, Rupert Brooke, or T. S. Eliot, some reflection of the experiments of Donne. Even Dryden and Pope were not above using the images of Donne. Ever since he widened the boundaries of poetic symbolism, we may be sure that he has been a living influence for original and fresh imagery, an exemplar of what Sacheverell Sitwell calls "the oft-concealed truth that poetry is, in great part, the art of metaphor." [1]

As I have already said so much on this subject, I shall merely add here a word on what Professor Saintsbury calls "the search for the after-sense, for contingent and secondary suggestion." [2] In Donne this search has a curious likeness to the inventions of the Symbolists, which have proved so expert in rendering complex sensations, in presenting the emotion merged with the idea and both bound up with the scene which provokes them. This is the picture of the poetic mind which Baudelaire gives us, and it has certain close resemblances to Donne's sensuous thinking. If we compare his use of symbols with the allegorical art of Quarles, his resemblance to Baudelaire becomes clearer. The allegory of Quarles is an

1. *All Summer in a Day*, p. 89.
2. *Short History of English Literature*, p. 412.

intellectual element made very evident; it is the expression of ideas by images. But Donne's symbolism gives to images the impression of ideas; it is a subtler and more living art. This art in Donne becomes purer when the symbol appears less willed by the author than divined by the reader, or more like music and less like arithmetic. It is this after-sense or overtone of thought in his image that gives peculiar power to his Metaphysical suggestion, and brings him close to the indirection of modern symbolism.

If poetry must continue to grow in intellectual content, it may still learn something from the imagery of Donne. So powerful was sensuous thinking in him that we may be sure that he chose fresh epithets and fresh metaphors, not so much because they were new, as because the old had ceased to convey a physical thing and had become abstract counters. He knew the truth which Mr. T. E. Hulme has put thus:

Fancy is not mere decoration added on to plain speech. Plain speech is essentially inaccurate. It is only by new metaphors, that is, by fancy, that it can be made precise.[1]

This is the truth that Dr. Johnson forgot when he condemned the Metaphysical poets for their pursuit of the new and strange.

In a special sense the Donne tradition holds an anxious interest for our age: it represents the poetry of that past age which was most like our own. Then, as now, poetry felt its beliefs crumbling beneath it.

1. *Speculations*, p. 137.

The problem of achieving order out of chaos lay heavily upon its music. A complex and difficult age called for a complex and difficult poetry that would be adequate and sincere in resolving a troubled soul. Scepticism was cooling the youthful blood of the Renascence, equivocation was slipping an interval between the mind and the senses, while disillusion was poisoning the emotions and sapping the vital force. But if the age had little to do with sincerity in the practical sense, the magnificent genius of Donne brought its poetry to the much more difficult sincerity of reproducing the exact curve of its feeling. Donne brought its poetry to meet T. E. Hulme's test of the highest verse:

It isn't the scale or kind of emotion produced that decides, but this one fact: Is there any real zest in it? Did the poet have an actually realised visual object before him in which he delighted? It doesn't matter if it were a lady's shoe or the starry heavens.[1]

In Donne's poetry it is first the lady's shoe, and then the starry heavens; but always there is an actually realized object before him. The object may be death, and his zest may be savage or terrible; but the object of the verse will be as actually realized and the zest as intense as the shroud which he wore for his last portrait. In all the perplexed ways of his life, he struggled with a demon of expression that never rested till even the sick-bed had surrendered the ghost of its meaning, and till he himself was "coming

1. *Op. cit.*, p. 137.

to that Holy room" where he was to make his final
music. In a word, he is a profound study in the discipline of the poetic mind, in the tension required to
force language into vital meaning; where Coleridge
failed at last, Donne succeeded, though at the expense
of some harmony. With similar problems before us,
we may look to him for instruction and encourage-
ment.

Donne belongs with those poets who have admit-
ted more than the usual amount of brain or indirect
expression into their poetry; with Browning and
Meredith, Baudelaire and Mallarmé. In our time
poets like T. S. Eliot and Paul Valéry, who share
Donne's interest in science and occupation with the
unity of the mind, have written verse which shows
that poetry of the type of Donne's has still to be
reckoned with. Read Valéry's *Serpent*, or let me
quote from Eliot's *Waste Land*:

> I have heard the key
> Turn in the door once and turn once only
> We think of the key, each in his prison
> Thinking of the key, each confirms a prison
> Only at nightfall, aethereal rumours
> Revive for a moment a broken Coriolanus.[1]

This is more like the *felt* thought and after-sense of
Donne than many critics would care to admit; mani-
festly it is in the direction of more brain, and belongs
to the same tradition of poetry.

In short, as we look back over the range of poetry

1. *Poems 1909–1925*, p. 84.

since Donne, we feel the truth of T. S. Eliot's re-mark:

Some one said: "The dead writers are remote from us because we *know* so much more than they did." Precisely, and they are that which we know.

Finally, a critical view of the Donne tradition im-poses two obligations: one, to remove the "meta-physical" arras from seventeenth-century poetry; the other, to regard Donne and his disciples in the com-pany of their peers.

APPENDICES

APPENDIX A

A CHRONOLOGY OF INHERITANCE

THE dates of "arrival" are at best approximate, but they try to give the year of the author's decisive appearance as a lyric poet and a possible influence. Publication is taken as the surest guide, though a faulty one in this century. Many of the "arrivals" could be put earlier; few, later.

Arrival	Author		Reason for Appearance
1600	Chapman	1559–1634	*Ovid's Banquet* quoted over 25 times in *England's Parnassus.*
1611	Donne	1573–1631	*An Anatomy of the World.*
1616	Jonson	1572–1637	*Works:* "Epigrams," "The Forest."
1630	E. Herbert	1583–1648	"Ode upon a Question." Elegy on Prince Henry, 1612. *Poems,* 1665.
1631	Townshend *fl.*	1601–1643	*Albion's Triumph.* Succeeded Jonson as Court writer of masques.
1633	G. Herbert	1593–1632	*The Temple.*
1633	King	1592–1669	Elegy on Donne, on Gustavus Adolphus. Editor of Donne? *Poems,* 1657.
1635	Quarles	1592–1644	*Emblemes.*
1638	Godolphin	1610–1643	Verses for Sandy's *Paraphrase*; for Donne in 1635; for Lady Rich.
1640	Carew	1595–1639	*Poems.* Edited by Townshend?
1642	Kynaston	1587–1642	"Cynthiades" in *Leoline and Sydanis.*
1646	Suckling	1609–1642	*Fragmenta Aurea.*

Arrival	*Author*		*Reason for Appearance*
1646	Crashaw	1613–1649	*Steps to the Temple.*
1646	J. Hall	1627–1656	*Poems.*
1647	Cowley	1618–1667	*The Mistress.*
1647	Cleveland	1613–1658	*A London Diurnal, with Several Select Poems.*
1649	Lovelace	1618–1658	*Lucasta.*
1650	Vaughan	1621–1695	*Silex Scintillans.*
1651	Stanley	1625–1678	*Poems.*
1652	Marvell	1621–1678	Wrote his best lyrics at Nun Appleton in 1650–52. *Poems,* 1681.
1652	Benlowes	1603–1676	*Theophila.*
1681	Dryden	1631–1700	*Absalom, Mac Flecknoe, The Medal.*

APPENDICES 253

APPENDIX B

SEVENTEENTH-CENTURY EDITIONS OF DONNE'S POETRY

ANNIVERSARIES

1. AN ANATOMY OF THE WORLD. London. Printed for Samuel Macham. An. Dom. 1611.
2. FIRST AND SECOND ANNIVERSARIES. London. Printed by M. Bradwood for S. Macham, 1612.
3. FIRST AND SECOND ANNIVERSARIES. London. Printed by A. Mathewes for Tho: Dewe, 1621.
4. FIRST AND SECOND ANNIVERSARIES. London. Printed by W. Stansby for Tho. Dewe, 1625.

COLLECTED POEMS

1. POEMS. Title: Poems, by J. D. with elegies on the authors death. London. Printed by M. F. for John Marriot, 1633.
2. POEMS. London. Printed by M. F. for John Marriot, 1635.
3. POEMS. London. Printed by M. F. for John Marriot, 1639.
4. POEMS. London. Printed by M. F. for John Marriot, 1649.
5. POEMS. London. Printed for John Marriot, 1650.
6. POEMS. London. Printed by J. Flesher, 1654.
7. POEMS. In the Savoy. Printed by T. N. for Henry Herringman, 1669.

OTHER EDITIONS

1. SATIRES. An edition was brought out in 1662. (See Nethercot, Jour. Eng. and Ger. Philol., 23 [1924], 178.)
2. HUYGHENS'S KORENBLOEMEN. Koren-bloemen. Nederlandsche gedichten Van Constantin Huyghens Ridder . . . Tweede druck . . . t'Amstelredam . . . 1672.

NOTE: All of these editions, except the Satires, may be verified in Keynes' *Bibliography of John Donne*. Professor Nethercot is my authority for the edition of the Satires.

APPENDIX C

CONCEITS IN CHAPMAN

THE style of Chapman, although "full and heightened" as Webster called it, shows a really "metaphysical" use of the conceit. To the samples which I have collected here, the reader should add an examination of Chapman's "Hymn to Christ upon the Cross," a comparison of the two parts of "Hero and Leander," and a perusal of "The Revenge." This study will be more illuminating if it is connected with Charles Crawford's "Montaigne, Webster, and Marston: Donne and Webster," in *Collectanea, Second Series.*

Ovid's Banquet of Sense:

(The page and column references are to *The Works of Chapman: Minor Poems*, London, 1874.)

> Whose ardour curl'd the foreheads of the trees,
> And made his green-love burn in his desire;   22–1

> Trusting herein his constellation,
> Ruled by love's beams, which Julia's eyes erected,
> Whose beauty was the star his life directed.   24–1

> My life that in my flesh a chaos is
> Should to a golden world be thus digested;   25–2

> Odour in heat and dryness is consite;
> Love, then a fire, is much thereto affected;
> And as ill smells do kill his appetite,
> With thankful savours it is still protected.   27–1

> She lay, and seem'd a flood of diamant
> Bounded in flesh; as still as Vesper's hair,
> When not an aspen-leaf is stirr'd with air.   29–2

> Betwixt mine eye and object, certain lines
> Move in the figure of a pyramis,
> Whose chapter in mine eye's gray apple shines
> The base within my sacred object is;   30–2

And as a taper burning in the dark —
As if it threaten'd every watchful eye
That viewing burns it — makes that eye his mark
And hurls gilt darts at it continually,   31–1

And there is contact not by application
Of lips or bodies, but of bodies' virtues,
As in our elemental nation
    Stars by their powers, which are their heat and light,
Do heavenly works,   34–2

    Sweet touch, the engine that love's bow doth bend,   37–1

A Coronet for his Mistress Philosophy:

And lovers kindling your enraged fires
At Cupid's bonfires burning in the eye,   38–1

Arranging in the army of her face
All virtue's forces,   39–1

And as a purple tincture given to glass,
    By clear transmission of the sun doth taint
    Opposed subjects; so my mistress' face
    Doth reverence in her viewers' brows depaint,   39–1

Bussy D'Ambois:

(The act, scene, and line references are to *Bussy D'Ambois and The Revenge*, Boas ed., Belles Lettres Series, Boston, 1905.)

Like bonfires of contributorie wood   II–i–44
Every mans look shew'd, fed with eithers spirit;
As one had beene a mirror to another,
Like formes of life and death each took from other;

D'Ambois (that like a lawrell put in fire   II–i–69
Sparkl'd and spit)

But D'Ambois sword (that lightned as it flew)   II–i–81
Shot like a pointed comet at the face

Who kneeling in the warme life of his friends,   II–i–134
(All freckled with the blood his rapier raind)

　　　　　　　　　　your selfe must seeme　　II–ii–197
The only agent, and the first orbe move
In this our set and cunning world of love.

Humour (that is the charriot of our food　　II–ii–238
In every body) must in them be fed,

I, every thought in our false clock of life　　III–i–75
Oft times inverts the whole circumference:

O, tis a subtle knave; how like the plague　　III–ii–15
Unfelt he strikes into the braine of man,

Or pluck'd one stick out of the golden faggot　　III–ii–104
In which the world of Saturne bound our lives,
Had all beene held together with the nerves,
The genius, and th' ingenious soule of D'Ambois.

　　　　　　　　　　his advanced valour　　III–ii–382
Is like a spirit rais'd without a circle,
Endangering him that ignorantly rais'd him,

　　　　　　　　　　a sudden night　　IV–i–162
Flowes through my entrailes, and a headlong chaos
Murmurs within me, which I must digest,

Till all at once the close mines of my heart　　IV–ii–180
Rise at full date, and rush into his bloud:
Ile bind his arme in silk, and rub his flesh
To make the veine swell, that his soule may gush
Into some kennell where it longs to lie;

A politician must, like lightning, melt　　IV–ii–192
The very marrow, and not taint the skin:
His wayes must not be seene; the superficies
Of the greene Center must not taste his feet,

Hereafter! t is a suppos'd infinite　　V–i–62
That from this point will rise eternally.

Then cut him up, and with my soules beams search　　V–i–81
The cracks and cavernes of his braine, and study
The errant wildernesse of a womans face,
Where men cannot get out, for all the comets
That have beene lighted at it.

V-iii-3

What violent heat is this? me thinks the fire
Of twenty lives doth on a suddaine flash
Through all my faculties:

And strike away this heartlesse trance of anguish: V-iv-2
Be like the sunne, and labour in eclipses.

Joine flames with Hercules, and when thou set'st   V-iv-149
Thy radiant forehead in the firmament,
Make the vast chrystall crack with thy receipt;

And as this taper, though it upwards look,   V-iv-209
Downwards must needs consume, so let our love!

Now turne from me, as here I turne from thee;   V-iv-219
And may both points of heavens strait axletree
Conjoyne in one, before thy self and me!

In the *Sacred Wood*, p. 20, Mr. T. S. Eliot first urged the likeness between Chapman and Donne. Professor Schoell evidently had not seen this page when he wrote page seven of his own *Études sur l'humanisme*. Mr. Eliot says:

"The man who wrote

      Guise, O my lord, how shall I cast from me
      The bands and coverts hindering me from thee?
      The garment or the cover of the mind
      The humane soul is; of the soul, the spirit
      The proper robe is; of the spirit, the blood;
      And of the blood, the body is the shroud:

and

      Nothing is made of nought, of all things made,
      Their abstract being a dream but of a shade,

is unquestionably kin to Donne." But turn to the book itself.

APPENDIX D

BIBLIOGRAPHY

THIS bibliography contains a selected list of the editions and works of most value to a student of this poetry. Some works not actually cited are included as background for the period. Only short titles are given.

I. EDITIONS

CAREW, THOMAS
The Poems of Thomas Carew. Ed. Arthur Vincent. Muses' Library. London, 1899.

CAROLINE POETS
Minor Poets of the Caroline Period. Ed. George Saintsbury. Oxford, 1905–21. 3 vols.

CHAPMAN, GEORGE
The Works of George Chapman: Poems and Minor Translations. Introduction by A. C. Swinburne. London, 1874.
Bussy D'Ambois and The Revenge. Ed. F. S. Boas. Belles Lettres Series. Boston, 1905.

CLEVELAND, JOHN
The Poems of John Cleveland. Ed. J. M. Berdan. New Haven, 1911.

COWLEY, ABRAHAM
The Poems of Abraham Cowley. Ed. A. R. Waller. Cambridge, 1905.

CRASHAW, RICHARD
The Poems of Richard Crashaw. Ed. L. C. Martin. Oxford, 1927.

DONNE, JOHN
The Poems of John Donne. Ed. H. J. C. Grierson. (Vol. i, Text and Appendixes.) Oxford, 1912. 2 vols.
Letters to Severall Persons of Honour. Ed. C. E. Merrill, Jr. New York, 1910.

Devotions. Ed. John Sparrow. Cambridge, 1923.
Paradoxes and Problemes. Nonesuch Press, 1923.
Donne's Sermons. Ed. L. P. Smith. Oxford, 1919.

DRYDEN, JOHN
The Poems of John Dryden. Ed. John Sargeaunt. Oxford, 1910.

HERBERT, GEORGE
The English Works of George Herbert. Ed. G. H. Palmer. Boston and New York, 1905. 3 vols.

HERBERT, LORD
The Poems of Lord Herbert of Cherbury. Ed. G. C. Moore Smith. Oxford, 1923.

JONSON, BEN
The Works of Ben Jonson. Vol. iii. Ed. Francis Cunningham (Gifford edition revised). London, 1910.

KING, HENRY
The English Poems of Henry King. Ed. Lawrence Mason. New Haven, 1914.

LOVELACE, RICHARD
The Poems of Richard Lovelace. Ed. C. H. Wilkinson. Oxford, 1925. 2 vols.

MARVELL, ANDREW
The Poems and Letters of Andrew Marvell. Ed. H. M. Margoliouth. Oxford, 1927. 2 vols.

METAPHYSICAL POETRY: DONNE TO BUTLER
Metaphysical Lyrics and Poems of the Seventeenth Century. Ed. H. J. C. Grierson. Oxford, 1921.

SUCKLING, SIR JOHN
The Works of Sir John Suckling. Ed. A. H. Thompson. London, 1910.

TOWNSHEND, AURELIAN
Aurelian Townshend's Poems and Masks. Ed. E. K. Chambers. Oxford, 1912.

VAUGHAN, HENRY
The Works of Henry Vaughan. Ed. L. C. Martin. Oxford, 1914. 2 vols.

II. Works

ALDEN, R. M.
In Studies in Philology, vol. xiv, no. 2, pp. 129–152: "The Lyrical Conceits of the Elizabethans."

BEECHING, H. C.
Introduction to The Poems of Richard Crashaw. Muses' Library. London, 1905.
Introduction to The Poems of Henry Vaughan. Muses' Library. London, 1896.

BREDVOLD, L. I.
In Journal of English and Germanic Philology, xxii (1923), 471–502: "The Naturalism of Donne in Relation to Some Renaissance Traditions."
In Studies in Shakespeare, Milton and Donne (New York, 1925): "The Religious Thought of Donne in Relation to Medieval and Later Traditions."

BRIGGS, W. D.
In Modern Philology, xv (Sept., 1917), 85–120: "Source-Material for Jonson's Underwoods and Miscellaneous Poems."
In Modern Language Notes, xlii, no. 6 (June, 1927), 404–411: Review of Herford and Simpson's Ben Jonson, vols. i–ii.

CAMBRIDGE HISTORY OF ENGLISH LITERATURE
In vol. iv (New York, 1910): Chap. 11, "John Donne," by H. J. C. Grierson. Chap. 12, "The English Pulpit from Fisher to Donne," by Rev. F. E. Hutchinson.
In vol. vii (New York, 1911): Chap. 1, "Cavalier Lyrists," by F. W. Moorman. Chap. 2, "The Sacred Poets," by Rev. F. E. Hutchinson. Chap. 4, "Lesser Caroline Poets," by George Saintsbury. Chap. 7, "John Bunyan. Andrew Marvell," by Rev. John Brown.

COLERIDGE, S. T.
Biographia Literaria. Everyman's Library. London, 1906.

COLLINS, J. C.
Introduction to The Poems of Lord Herbert of Cherbury. London, 1881.

COURTHOPE, W. J. A.
  History of English Poetry. Vol. iii. London, 1903.

CRAWFORD, CHARLES
  Collectanea, Second Series. Stratford-on-Avon, 1907.

DICTIONARY OF NATIONAL BIOGRAPHY
  See for brief accounts of the poets in the Donne tradition.

DOWDEN, EDWARD
  In New Studies in Literature (Boston and New York, 1895),
  pp. 90–120: "The Poetry of John Donne."

DRYDEN, JOHN
  Essays of John Dryden. Ed. W. P. Ker. Oxford, 1900. 2 vols.

ELIOT, T. S.
  Homage to John Dryden. London, 1924.
  The Sacred Wood. London, 1920.
  In The Dial, vol. lxxxiv, no. 3 (March, 1928), pp. 246–250:
  "The Poems of Richard Crashaw."
  In The Dial, vol. lxxxiii, no. 3 (Sept., 1927), pp. 259–263:
  "The Silurist."
  In The Nation and Athenaeum, xxxiii (9 June, 1923), 331–332:
  "John Donne."
  In The New Statesman, viii (3 March, 1917), 518–519: "Re-
  flections on Vers Libre."

FLETCHER, J. G.
  In The Saturday Review of Literature (27 August, 1927), pp.
  65–66: "Two Elements in Poetry."

GOSSE, EDMUND
  The Life and Letters of John Donne. London, 1899. 2 vols.
  More Books on the Table. New York, 1923.

GOURMONT, REMY DE
  Decadence. Translated by W. A. Bradley. European Library.
  New York, 1921.

GRIERSON, H. J. C.
  The Poems of John Donne. vol. ii: Introduction and Commentary. Oxford, 1912.
  The First Half of the Seventeenth Century. New York, 1906.
  In Review of English Studies, vol. ii, no. 8 (Oct., 1926): Review
  of Praz's Secentismo e Marinismo in Inghilterra. (See also
  the Cambridge History, vol. iv, chap. 11.)

HARRISON, J. S.
Platonism in English Poetry of the Sixteenth and Seventeenth
Centuries. New York, 1903.

HERFORD, C. H., AND PERCY SIMPSON
Ben Jonson. Vol. ii. Oxford, 1925.

HOBBES, THOMAS
Leviathan. London, George Routledge & Sons Ltd., n. d.

HULME, T. E.
Speculations. Edited by Herbert Read. London, 1924.

JESSOPP, A.
John Donne. London, 1897.

JOHNSON, SAMUEL
Lives of the English Poets. World's Classics. Oxford, 1906.
2 vols.

KEYNES, GEOFFREY
Bibliography of John Donne. Cambridge, 1914.

LEA, KATHLEEN M.
In Modern Language Review, vol. xx, no. 4 (Oct., 1925), pp.
389–406: "Conceits."

LEGOUIS, EMILE
History of English Literature 650–1660. New York, 1926.
(Translated by Helen D. Irvine.)

LUCAS, F. L.
Authors Dead and Living. London, 1926.

MELTON, W. F.
The Rhetoric of John Donne's Verse. Baltimore, 1906.

MURRY, J. M.
Keats and Shakespeare. London, Oxford, 1925.

NETHERCOT, A. H.
In Journal of English and Germanic Philology, xxiii (1924),
173–198: "The Reputation of the 'Metaphysical Poets'
during the Seventeenth Century."
In Philological Quarterly, vol. iv, no. 2 (1925), pp. 161–179:
"The Reputation of the 'Metaphysical Poets' during the
Age of Pope."

PRAZ, MARIO
Secentismo e Marinismo in Inghilterra. Firenze, 1925.

RAMSAY, M. P.
Les doctrines médiévales chez Donne. Oxford, 1916.

READ, HERBERT
In The Criterion, vol. i, no. 3 (April, 1923), pp. 246–266: "The Nature of Metaphysical Poetry."

REED, E. B.
English Lyrical Poetry. New Haven, 1912.

SAINTSBURY, GEORGE
History of English Prosody. Vol. ii. London, 1923.
Introduction to Poems of John Donne. Muses' Library. London, 1896.
Short History of English Literature. New York, 1907. (See also the Cambridge History, vol. vii, chap. 4.)

SCHELLING, F. E.
English Literature during the Lifetime of Shakespeare. Revised Edition. New York, 1927.

SCHOELL, F. L.
Études sur l'humanisme continental en Angleterre. Paris, 1926.

SIMPSON, E. M.
A Study of the Prose Works of John Donne. Oxford, 1924.

SIMPSON, PERCY. See Herford, C. H.

SOCIETY FOR PURE ENGLISH
Tract XI: Metaphor i, by E. B. Clarendon Press, 1922.

SPINGARN, J. E.
Critical Essays of the Seventeenth Century. Ed. J. E. Spingarn. Oxford, 1908. 3 vols.

SWINBURNE, A. C.
A Study of Ben Jonson. London, 1889.
Contemporaries of Shakespeare. Ed. Gosse and Wise. London, 1919.

VAN DOREN, MARK
The Poetry of John Dryden. New York, 1920.

WALTON, IZAAK
Lives. Morley's Universal Library. London, 1888.

WELLS, HENRY W.
Poetic Imagery. New York, 1924.

WENDELL, BARRETT
The Temper of the Seventeenth Century in Literature. New York, 1904.